That Magic Mile

The National Championship at Du Quoin 1948-1970

By Thomas Nasti

That Magic Mile
The National Championship at Du Quoin 1948-1970

Text – Thomas Nasti
Editor – Stacy Faye Bleyer
Design & Layout – Ian Weidner

ISBSN 0-9703401-0-9

Published by The Etherton Group
© 1997 Thomas Nasti. All rights reserved. No part of this publication may be reproduced, stored in a retrieval system or transmitted in any form or by any means – electronic, mechanical, photocopying, recording or otherwise – without prior written permission of the copyright owner or publisher.

This book is dedicated to my parents, Jim and Jane, who always thought automobile racing was just so much "Tomfoolery."

Introduction

The first automobile race held in the United States took place between Chicago and Evanston, Illinois, on Thanksgiving Day of 1895, beginning a tradition of motorsports in the state that would last until the present. The round-trip, nine hour contest was sponsored by the Chicago Times Herald newspaper and was won by Frank Duryea of Peoria, a pioneer automobile maker. Duryea piloted a gasoline powered vehicle to victory over five other cars at a then blistering speed of five miles per hour.

By 1909 racing automobiles was the new sport in America. There were only about 30,000 registered vehicles in the country at that time. Most of the population did not own cars so it was no doubt fascinating to see the "horseless carriages" roaring loudly down the few suitable roadways.

That same year, the first race was held on the massive, tar and crushed stone surfaced 2.5-mile oval track at Indianapolis. Not yet the 500-mile classic that it would become in 1911, the 250-mile race was part of the recently formed American Automobile Association's National Driving Championship, 24-race calendar. The race was won by Bob Burman in a Buick "Bug" at the speed of 55.5 miles per hour.

In 1910, 19 races sanctioned by the AAA counted toward the championship. Three of them were held on a road course in Elgin, outside of Chicago, and were won respectively by Dave Buick, driving a Marmon in the first race of 170-miles; Al Livingstone took the 230-miler in a National while Ralph Mulford clinched the 305-mile contest in a Lozier. Elgin would host 13 more national championship races until 1915, all in excess of 150 miles.

In 1914, when Illinois began the construction of "hard roads," Galesburg became the next location used for an AAA race. It was a 100-mile dirt affair won by Mulford, this time in a Duesenberg at a speed of 64.5 mph. Eddy O'Donnell would win the following year's 100-mile dirt race, also in a Duesenberg.

Chicago hosted two AAA races in 1915, and in June, Englishman Dario Resta won a grueling 500-mile board track race in a Peugeot, coming close to the magic 100-mph barrier with a speed of 97.5 mph. Resta would return to the same track less than two months later and conquer the century mark with a firm 101.8 mph clocking, this time in a 100-mile event.

The following year, Resta became the first driver to win both the Indianapolis 500 and the AAA's National Driving Championship in the same year.

Championship racing stayed in Chicago until 1918, despite America's entry into World War I. The action then returned to Elgin and lasted until 1920. For the next 13 years the closest championship racing to be seen by an Illinois fan was in the neighboring state of Indiana, at the Indianapolis Motor Speedway, which had been paved with bricks in 1911. By this time the annual Memorial Day race was firmly entrenched as the AAA's premier event.

By 1933, the sanctioning body's calendar had dwindled to just three races, largely due to the economic effects of the Depression; but "Indy" continued even though more races were needed to keep the sport alive. The following year another race was added to the schedule. It would be held in the Illinois capital of Springfield, the site of the annual state fair since 1894. The inaugural 100-mile race was won by the appropriately named driver, Billy Winn, who averaged just over 77 mph in a Stokely Special. Also, the race was attended by well over 20,000 people. Obviously, Illinois fans had been starving to see a race for the past 14 years.

Springfield's annual 100-mile race has now been run more than 60 times, but it went through some lean years. Held the following year, with Winn taking the checkered flag again, the race was dropped from the AAA's championship schedule in 1936 simply because the governing body demanded too large a purse from the promoters. Races were still held; however, they did not count towards the AAA title. And, a few years later, the world again found itself involved in a global conflict which put a temporary end to racing everywhere. AAA sanctioned racing would not return to Springfield until August of 1948. That same year, a small town in the coal country of Southern Illinois would also become the site of AAA national championship racing. That town is Du Quoin.

That Magic Mile

Good Enough For Two
September 4, 1948

Du Quoin is a city of over 6,000 friendly people located in Perry County, in the southwest portion of the state.

The town was named after John Du Quoigne, a literate chief of the Kaskaskia Indian tribe. Much of the city's origin and future was due to the laying of track by the Illinois Central Railroad in the early 1850's.

The city was mapped out in 1853 by William Richart, the county surveyor, and the following year buildings were erected by the railroad along both Main and Washington streets. Today they are still the main thoroughfares in the city.

A major railway link, along with the abundance of coal (which was the region's major industry for decades to come), caused the town to grow rapidly. In July of 1857, an election was called and a mayor and police magistrate were put into office.

In 1871, Du Quoin resident Tom Hayes, a coal miner by trade who also operated a livery stable, began a sideline soda water business. But in 1883, Hayes died in a mine accident and left both the stable and soda businesses to his wife, Mary, and son William, who was born in 1877.

His wife looked after the family concerns and they prospered. In 1882, Mary Hayes was listed as the only female proprietor of any of the many businesses that had located in Du Quoin. Young William began working in the soda business at an early age and sold the carbonated water to the townsfolk from a wheelbarrow.

In 1906, a new bottling plant was erected just north of the city's southern boundary. And, by 1913, William, having undertaken the day-to-day operation of the soda business, landed the lucrative franchise rights to sell Coca Cola in the Du Quoin area and many of the sur-

William R. Hayes
(Courtesy of Jane Rader)

rounding counties. Hayes later established a dairy business and was the co-owner of a string of Southern Illinois movie theaters.

A side from being an astute and successful businessman, William R. Hayes had a vision. That vision became reality in 1923 when, under his direction, the first of many Du Quoin Fairs was held on a 30-acre site, located next to the bottling plant. Along with the many attractions and sideshows at the fair there was also a 3,000-seat grandstand which fronted a half-mile dirt, horse racing oval.

In 1924, electric lights were added to the fair grounds; and, in 1929 the six-year-old fair was the first in the country to present a nighttime stage show. Despite his conservative demeanor, Hayes obviously possessed a distinct flare for show business. In 1931, the fair began to develop on a massive scale with the purchase of 800 acres of strip mined land from the Black Gold Coal Company, adjacent to the existing fair grounds.

By 1940, most of the bare, scarred earth had been reclaimed, numerous trees had been planted and there was the addition of several man-made lakes which transformed Hayes' fairground into a truly scenic and opulent setting.

Along with developing his own fair, Hayes served for years as one of the directors of the annual state fair that was held in Springfield.

When the Illinois State Fair opened, its one-mile, oval dirt track was one of its premier attractions and thousands of people attended the horse races and other demonstrations that were held before the covered grandstand. In 1905, the great daredevil driver, Barney Oldfield, entertained the crowd by taking lap after lap in his Peerless Green Dragon car. Oldfield returned again to Springfield in 1910 and drove a Blitzen Benz in a special match race against an airplane. Oldfield lost when his car overturned; but, fortunately, he was not injured.

The Du Quoin Fair also had been holding horse races for years and although Hayes' first sporting passion was that of harness racing, he also understood the entertainment value that automobile racing provided. It had been successful at the state fair and at his annual fair, as year after year people crowded around the Du Quoin track to watch the exhibition races that were held.

In 1945 the original grandstand at Du Quoin burned to the ground. Plans were made to erect a new one that would provide 10,000 spectators with the luxury of an unobstructed view of the entire one-mile oval dirt track, which also was penned for construction.

The main entrance to the fairgrounds in 1923. (Courtesy of Randall Harbuck, C.C.P.)

The new grandstand and track were completed by the end of 1947 and early the following year application was made to the AAA for the Du Quoin Fair to host a 100-mile national championship race. After a visit by the sanctioning body's contest board to inspect the new track for safety reasons, permission was granted for not only one race, but two. The first was scheduled for September 4, 1948, and the second was a season-ending contest on October 10. Both races awarded points counting toward the AAA National Driver's Championship.

By 1948, the AAA's championship calendar had been rejuvenated and regained its former prominence, listing 10 events besides the Indianapolis 500. These included 100-mile races at Dallas and Langhorne, Pennsylvania. Springfield, Milwaukee and Atlanta, along with Du Quoin, would each hold two races. One of the Milwaukee events would be 200 miles in distance and would be run on August 29, a week before the first running of the big cars at Du Quoin.

The original grandstand was erected in 1923 and seated 3,000 fans. It burned to the ground in 1945. (Courtesy of Randall Harbuck, C.C.P.)

Construction of the new grandstand, along with a one-mile dirt oval racetrack was completed in 1947. (Courtesy of The Southern Illinoisan)

That Magic Mile

The first race promised to be a barn-burner, as 10 of the top Indianapolis 500 drivers had entered. Hayes had recruited Sam Nunis, a veteran auto racing promoter from Trenton, New Jersey, to insure that the show would go on without a hitch. Popular driver, Ted Horn, the reigning two-time national champion on his way to an unprecedented third consecutive title, was the first to officially enter. At that time, Horn was the most consistent money winner in Indianapolis 500 history, even though he had never won the prestigious race. Out of nine starts he had finished second once, third four times and in the fourth position three times. His worst showing was 16th in 1935, his rookie year at the speedway. With a win at Dallas in April, and at Springfield less than three weeks prior to the Du Quoin race, he would be one of the speedsters to watch.

Other drivers expected to provide a strong showing included Tony Bettenhausen and Myron Fohr, who had just teamed to win the 200-miler at Milwaukee, and Chicago's Emil Andres, the winner of the 100-mile June event at Milwaukee. There was Johnny Mantz, victor of the 100-lap August race also held at Milwaukee, and Walt Brown, who stole the 100-mile show in June at Langhorne.

Mauri Rose, who had won the Indianapolis 500 for the last two years, did not enter. He intended to concentrate only on the 500 for the remainder of his career.

But Bill Holland, Rose's Blue Crown teammate and runner up in the 1948 Indy 500 entered, as did Rex Mays, the 1940-41 national champion who had finished third in the final AAA standings in 1947. Mays was also in possession of the current one-mile dirt track world record of 33.7 seconds set at Langhorne in June, and at that time, the only four-time pole position qualifier for the Indianapolis 500. Other hot shoes scheduled to appear included Hal Robson, Charlie Van Acker, Paul Russo, Spider Webb, and Lee Wallard. Wallard had impressed racing fans on Memorial Day by qualifying fifth and finishing seventh in his first appearance at Indianapolis.

Rex Mays sat in the pole position for the first race at Du Quoin with a qualifying speed of 99.972 mph. (Courtesy of the Indianapolis Motor Speedway)

The year's hot rookie, Johnnie Parsons, also entered. Parsons had made the move up from the midget racers to the big cars and finished second in his first championship grind at Springfield on August 21.

These drivers made up the bulk of the field of 21 men who would seek to qualify for the 18-car starting grid at Du Quoin and compete for the prestige of winning the inaugural event.

Qualifying began on schedule at noon in front of a packed grandstand, with thousands of other fans encircling the track under a blazing Southern Illinois sun. The dirt on the slightly banked track had been blended with tons of calcium chloride to keep dust thrown up by the cars to a minimum. Twenty cars made their qualifying attempts and

Mays leads the field on the pace lap. (The Bruce Craig Collection)

Ted Horn (1) passes Hal Robson (26) on the outside. Horn won an unprecedented third AAA national title after finishing third in the first race of 1948. (The Bruce Craig Collection)

California's rapid Rex Mays emerged as the pole sitter after laying down the day's fastest time of 36.01 seconds for a speed of 99.972 mph in the No. 5 Bowes Seal Fast Offenhauser. Tony Bettenhausen of Tinley Park, Illinois, driving the No. 16 Belanger Motors Special, would start the race in second with his time of 37.30. Third on the grid was Horn in "Beauty," the No. 1 emblazoned car he had constructed in his shop in Patterson, New Jersey.

The 18 Indianapolis-type racing cars faced flagman Bill Vandewaters' starting signal. The starting lineup behind Horn was Russo, Mel Hansen, Fohr, Wallard, Parsons, Van Acker, Bill Sheffler, Andres, Robson, George Lynch, Steve Truchan, Bill Cantrell, Charlie Rogers and Duke Dinsmore. Sam Nunis excercised his promoter's option and substituted alternate starter Floyd Davis to take over Spider Webb's position when the latter driver's engine failed to start.

When the green flag fell, Mays kept his position and led into the first turn followed by Bettenhausen, with Russo in close pursuit. But, before the end of the first lap, Bettenhausen took the lead. Mays had encountered engine problems and dropped out of the race. The formidable Russo also suffered mechnical woes during the first mile and retired with a broken clutch. But Mel Hansen was on the charge with Wallard hanging right on his tail. Hansen took the lead as Bettenhausen slowed to run in the middle of the pack. Hansen drove his Schafer Gear Special so hard he set a 25-mile speed record with a clocking of 15.18 minutes, but dropped out on lap 32 with a blown engine.

Wallard was in the right place at the right time and inherited the lead, but was pressured immediately by Fohr in the No. 32 Marchese and Horn. After holding off the two drivers, the former New York traffic cop opened up a secure lead and paced the field for the remaining incident-free 60 laps to win the race, along with the lion's share of the $10,000 purse. Wallard averaged 88.38 mph in 1 hr., 7 min., 53.28 seconds in his No. 12 Iddings Special to claim his first National Championship victory.

Lee Wallard won two AAA National Championship races during his career. The first victory came in the inuagural 100-mile event at Du Quoin. The second was at the Indianapolis 500 in 1951. (Courtesy of the Indianapolis Motor Speedway.)

Wallard was followed across the line by Fohr. Horn finished third and clinched the 1948 driver's championship as a result. Charlie Van Acker logged a fourth place finish in the Redmer Special and rounding out the top-five was Bill Sheffler in the Bromme Offy.

Two Cents Missing
October 10, 1948

In his headquarters at Du Quoin's St. Nicholas Hotel, promoter Sam Nunis was no doubt a happy man. The first race at Hayes' fairgrounds had been a huge success. Over 20,000 people had attended and Southern Illinois was cast into the national sporting spotlight. At a dollar a ticket, advance sales for Du Quoin's second event were brisk. Entries had been received from all the drivers who had competed in the September race along with a few extras. This increased the total of Indianapolis 500 veterans who would start at Du Quoin to 13. Andy Granatelli and son Vince brought their Grancor Special. It would be driven by Hal Cole, who had finished sixth at Indianapolis. Also entered to drive was Eddie Zaluki in the Auto Shippers Special. He had failed to qualify at this year's 500, but had finished a respectable seventh three weeks ago at Springfield.

Wallard was back to defend his title in the Iddings Special and was the first driver to enter the season's final championship encounter. He had placed sixth at Springfield despite starting from the pole. Myron Fohr also was returning. He had recently won the year's second Springfield race after inheriting the lead on lap 73 from Mel Hansen.

Qualifying began on time at 12:30 p.m.; and Rex Mays, true to his nature, again qualified on the pole with a speed of 98.173 mph. Hansen, now driving the No. 18 Truchan Offy qualified second. Paul Russo occupied the third position in the Belanger Special. He was substituting for his injured friend, Tony Bettenhausen, who had burned his left leg in a midget car race that had been added to the Du Quoin program and run a few days previously.

Ted Horn would start in fourth. It was a token appearance for Horn, as he had already won the 1948 driver's championship. Gerry, his wife of just 17 days, was in the packed grandstand to cheer him on. In 1948 AAA rules did not allow women into the pit or infield areas. At that time it was considered a bad omen within the totally male-dominated sport to let a woman anywhere near a racing car, until after it had won a race.

Rounding out the top seven qualifying positions were: Fohr, in fifth, piloting the Marchese Special; Johnny Mantz of California, in sixth in the No. 98 Agajanian Special; and Johnnie Parsons, in seventh driving the Kurtis Kraft.

Mays would be a contender. It was an all too well-known fact among the drivers that the best place to start any race was in the front row, and that's just where Mays was. At that time in his career he had secured 19 pole-position starts, more than any other active driver. He had led for 16 laps in the year's second race at Springfield before relinquishing the lead to Hansen.

When the green flag dropped on the 18 starting cars, Mays gave it all he had. But, just as in the first race at Du Quoin, his car suffered an engine problem and he dropped out immediately. Russo breezed past second place Hansen and took the lead before the end of the first lap. With the first mile in the record books, Russo began to build a comfortable lead as the cars headed down the backstretch.

As the cars roared through the north turns to complete the second lap, the left front spindle on Ted Horn's car failed, causing it to loose a wheel. The crowd fell silent as the champion's No. 1 machine went out of control and began to somersault violently through the air, hitting the car driven by Mantz.

Horn was thrown out of the flipping car and onto the track near the exit of the fourth turn with his car coming to rest in an upright position on the infield grass. Mantz's car also went out of control and flipped several times before his vehicle came to rest against the outside guardrail near the end of turn four. The race was immediately red flagged and both Horn and Mantz were rushed by ambulance to Du Quoin's Marshall Browning Hospital.

After winning the 1948 driver's championship, Ted Horn made a token appearance in the second race at Du Quoin that year. (The Bruce Craig Collection)

Mechanic, Charlie Simover, examines the wrecked car of Ted Horn. (The Bruce Craig Collection)

The car of Johnny Mantz is removed from the track. (Courtesy of Pierce & Sons Motors)

That Magic Mile

After Mantz's car was removed from the track and Horn's moved further into the infield, the race was restarted with Russo retaining his first place position. But, he could not hold his lead. Instead of building an advantage again, Russo was forced to give up his earlier domination. The lead changed hands several times between Russo and Johnnie Parsons. Finally, on lap 50, Parsons took command. He was never challenged thereafter and completed the race in 1 hour., 11 minutes., and 47.7 seconds. Runner-up was the tenacious Russo, followed by Bill Sheffler. Officially, Fohr was credited with fourth, but he had finally been overcome by his car's leaking exhaust fumes on lap 45, and had to be relieved by George Connor. Connor was available as a relief driver as he had failed to qualify for the race. Hal Cole took fifth in the Grancor Special and Eddie Zalucki improved on his Springfield finish and grabbed sixth.

Parsons' hard charging drive to the checkered flag gained him his first championship victory, but it was overshadowed by the sad news of Horn's death. The three-time national champion had been pronounced dead 20 minutes after his accident. He died as a result of severe head injuries, a crushed chest and multiple fractures to his left leg. Mantz was lucky. He had been released from the hospital almost immediately; surprisingly with only minor cuts and bruises.

The 38-year-old Horn is still recognized as one of America's greatest racing drivers and is considered by many to have been the highwater mark of racing professionalism. Today he is still ranked seventh among such notable drivers as A. J. Foyt, Al Unser and Rick Mears (all four-time Indianapolis winners), three-time winners Wilbur Shaw, Bobby Unser and Mauri Rose, along with two-time victors Roger Ward and Gordon Johncock as the top 10 points earners ever to drive at Indianapolis. Thus, Horn holds the distinction of being the only non-victor among that elite group of winners in the more than 80-year history of the fabled Indianapolis Motor Speedway.

Horn jokingly refered to the Indianapolis 500 as his "jinx assignment," and was reportedly a very superstitious individual. On the morning of his death, Horn shaved. He had not shaved on the day of a race for

Johnnie Parsons' first National Championship victory was overshadowed by the death of Ted Horn. (Courtesy of the Indianapolis Motor Speedway)

years. His recent bride worn a green dress. Horn considered the color bad luck. He was known to slip a dime in one shoe and two pennies in the other to bring himself luck while he raced. When his shoes were removed after his death at Marshall Browning Hospital, just one thin dime dropped to the floor.

So intent was Horn on winning at Indy that it caused the collapse of his first marriage early in 1948. His first wife, Theresa, claimed that she had separated from him because he insisted on competing in the most dangerous of sports until he had won the prestigious Indianapolis feature. But, Horn's career had been a relatively safe one at a time when racing cars were not the more technologically sophisticated and safer machines that they are today. During his career he had been seriously injured only once, which was during a race at Nashville, Tenn. He spent several months hospitalized before returning to competition.

Eylard "Ted" Horn's remarkable two-decade career in racing began in 1927 when he was a teenager employed as an apprentice photo engraver for a Los Angeles newspaper. It culminated with his becoming the first and last three time consecutive national champion. Horn logged close to 4,500 racing miles in 10 races at Indianapolis alone during his majestic career, compared to the all-time mileage leader, A.J. Foyt, who has driven an unbelievable 12,272 miles in his record 35 consecutive starts in the 500.

Horn first attempted to qualify for the 500 in 1934, but failed to make the field because his car wasn't fast enough. However, that same year he clinched the AAA's Pacific Coast Class B midget car championship.

In 1935 he moved east to Patterson, New Jersey and established "Ted Horn Engineering," becoming one of the few racing drivers of his time to design, construct and drive his own racing cars. That year he did qualify at Indianapolis in a Ford V-8 powered car and completed 145 laps before being sidelined because of a steering malfunction. He was credited with a 16th place finish out of the traditional starting field of 33 drivers.

In his next eight Indianapolis races Horn never finished lower than fourth. In 1947 he held down the pole position in the second of his three stints behind the wheel of Chicago labor leader, Mike Boyle's Maserati Tipo 8CTF.

Al Bloemaker, author of the book, "500 Miles To Go," wrote that Horn's former competitor and friend Mauri Rose, the winner of the 1947 speedway classic, admitted after the race that Horn had been the class of the field in that year's 500 saying, "Ted Horn drove the best race this year and I guess we all know it. He made four pit stops, I made only one, but Ted still finished third and posted the fastest laps of the race to do it."

At the time of his death, the affable Horn had six big car victories to his credit and held over 70 track records across the United States. Besides his three national titles, he was also the 1938-39 AAA Midwest Sprint Car champion and a three-time Eastern Division Sprint Car ace.

Three-time consecutive AAA National Champion (1946, 47 & 48), Ted Horn, was the first and only driver to meet death at Du Quoin.
(Courtesy of the Indianapolis Motor Speedway)

When recently retired Wilbur Shaw, the president of Indianapolis Motor Speedway, joined Lee Wallard, Bill Holland and three other racing drivers as pallbearers at Horn's funeral, he reflected on his former competitor and Maserati teammate saying of the deceased champion, "Ted was one of the finest gentlemen who ever sat behind the wheel of a racing car, and one of the world's greatest champions."

Horn was the first and last driver to meet his death on the Du Quoin oval. The following year, the race was named "The Ted Horn Memorial."

That Magic Mile

Charlie Van Acker finished fourth in the first race of 1948, but was sidelined after 65 laps in the second event. (The Bruce Craig Collection)

The Tinley Park Express
September 3, 1949

The 1949 race was a milestone in the history of the Du Quoin oval. For the first time an Indianapolis 500 winner would compete on the Southern Illinois clay. Bill Holland, who had finished second in his rookie year at the speedway in 1947, and second again in 1948, finally clinched the 500-miler in 1949 driving a front wheel drive Blue Crown Special for car owner Lou Moore. Cars owned by Moore had won the 500 for an unprecedented three consecutive years (1947-49) and twice before that.

But for Du Quoin, Holland was scheduled to drive the Marion Love Machine entry, which he had piloted to a fourth place finish on August 20th at Springfield. Johnnie Parsons, George Connor and Myron Fohr, the three drivers who had followed Holland across the Indy finish line (in that order) were also back. Mel Hansen, who had won the Springfield race in the ex-Rex Mays Bowes Seal Fast ride, also was returning to Du Quoin. Mays had switched to a new car for the 1949 season.

Parsons was leading the points chase for the national title after winning a 200-mile race at Milwaukee. He had driven the last two miles of the race with a flat tire, but still managed to beat the field to the checkered flag. Along with a victory in the season opening 100-mile race at Dallas, "Jittery Johnnie" looked to be the odds on favorite for the AAA's big car title.

Fohr was trailing Parsons by just 310 points, with Holland third in the standings and looking to put a national title along side his Indy trophy. At that time, the AAA's point system awarded as many as 200 points to the winner of a 100-mile event while a driver finishing in 18th place could collect four. With the six remaining races of the 1949 season scheduled for 100-miles each, many drivers still retained a mathematical chance of clinching the championship.

Another driver returning to Du Quoin was Tony Bettenhausen, who was entered in the experimental No. 99 Meyer & Drake Special. Two things made this car different from the rest of the 25 entries. It was smaller and lighter than the usual big car and it was powered by a supercharged Offenhauser midget car motor, the only one of its kind. The car had not fared well when introduced at Springfield, finishing in the 18th and last position. However, its poor showing wasn't the result of mechanical failure, but was caused when Bettenhausen burned his hand trying to straighten out a bent exhaust pipe after a slight collision with another car during the first lap, forcing him to retire from the event.

Other drivers entered for the third Du Quoin race included Lee Wallard, still driving the Iddings Special. Paul Russo was back, this time in a Tuffy's Offy, as was teammate Walt Brown, who had finished second to Parsons in the Milwaukee 200. Charlie Van Acker was returning in the Redmer Special and Emil Andres, who finished ninth at Indy, also came back to compete in the Schoof Special. Rookie big car driver Duane Carter also was ready to qualify for the first time at Du Quoin in a car formerly driven by Bettenhausen.

More that 15,000 fans were on hand when qualifications began at noon under a cloudless sky. Bettenhausen promptly went out and hung up a new track record with a 35.92-second clocking in the Meyer-Drake No. 99. Not only that, the Tinley Park, Illinois native passed another Du Quoin milestone and cracked the 100-mph barrier with a speed of 100.223, shattering Mays' pole speed of 99.972 set in qualifications for the first race of 1948. When time trials were over Bettenhausen sat firmly on the pole and it was obvious the little "experimental" car was going to be a force to be reckoned with.

The green flag dropped at 3:00 p.m. and Mel Hansen, starting in the second position, drove low into the first turn to emerge with the lead as he began his first trip down the backstretch. Bettenhausen was right on his tail and the Indy winner, "Wild Bill" Holland, was third.

That Magic Mile

Hansen maintained his domination over the field for the first 30 laps, but the new Bowes Seal Fast driver was paying the price for his lead. His right rear tire was losing tread fast and he was forced into the pits for fresh rubber, giving up the lead to Bettenhausen.

Hansen made a lightning fast pit stop and was back on the track in a flash. He began to catch up to the Meyer-Drake car, cutting down Bettenhausen's lead to three-quarters of a lap. Hansen was making time on the straightaways with his more powerful car, while Bettenhausen's lighter car went through the turns as if on rails. But, just as in the first race at Du Quoin, Hansen pushed his car so hard the engine expired.

Bettenhausen won his first race at Du Quoin and nailed the fifth big car victory of his career. He was followed across the finish line 41-seconds later by the steady driving Holland, with Connor driving the Granatelli entry to third. Wallard finished fourth.

Parsons finished an unusual eleventh in the Kurtis-Kraft machine, but won three of the remaining races that season to become the AAA's 1949 title winner. He would go on to win the Indianapolis 500 the following year.

Tony Bettenhausen led the last 70 laps of the 1949 Ted Horn Memorial and scored his first victory at Du Quoin. He also broke the 100-mph barrier for the first time on the oval during qualifications. Here he receives his trophy from Jane Hayes, the granddaughter of William R. Hayes. (Courtesy of Jane Rader)

"The B Train"
September 1 & 3, 1951

Rain prevented the running of the national championship big cars in 1950 and for the first time a scheduled stock car race on the Du Quoin mile. But the weather cooperated in 1951 and under the direction of St. Louis promoter Buck Kidd, who had replaced Sam Nunis, two big car races were scheduled for the last Saturday and Monday of fair week. A total of 26 drivers brought their cars to Southern Illinois to qualify. Saturday's race was to be a regular 100-mile event while the Labor Day event would be a first ever 200-miler at Du Quoin.

Lee Wallard would not be returning to Du Quoin. He had won the Indianapolis 500 substituting for Tony Bettenhausen in the No. 99 Meyer & Drake car, now owned by Indiana Chrysler dealer Murrell Belanger. Wallard, who had raced for years with little reward, qualified in the middle of the first row on Indy's starting grid and took over the lead on the 81st of 200 laps. Despite a broken exhaust system, a lost right-rear shock absorber, and no brakes during the final laps he managed to hold on for his only Indianapolis victory. Just four days later the 40-year old Wallard suffered terrible burns in a racing accident at Reading, Pennsylvania and would never race again.

Bettenhausen had decided to try his luck in the 1951 Indy 500 behind the wheel of the Mobil Oil car. It was the car driven to victory lane at Indianapolis by Bill Holland in 1949.

Unfortunately, Melvin Eugene Bettenhausen (Tony was a nickname) was never a factor in that year's Indy. By the time he had climbed from his ninth place starting position up into fifth only nine cars of the original 33 were still running. Bettenhausen spun out in the northwest turn on lap 178 and wound up becoming the 25th and final retirement in that year's attrition plagued 500.

At Du Quoin, Bettenhausen returned to the cockpit of the Belanger and was back in his element. Bettenhausen's true forte, after all, was the dirt tracks. After posting three big car victories out of six races he was a strong favorite to win the 1951 driver's championship. Bettenhausen's only threat midway through the season was from Walt Faulkner, who had won a 250-mile race at Darlington, South Carolina and the 200-miler at Milwaukee.

Along with returning Du Quoin veterans such as Bettenhausen, Parsons, Russo and Carter, many new drivers would attempt to qualify for their first race on the fairground's oval.

Newcomers included distance specialist Faulkner and the last year's national champion, Banks, who despite winning just one race in 1950, had accumulated enough top-10 finishes in the season's other 12 races to win the title crown. Among those joining Banks were Sam Hanks and Bill Vukovich, the respective 1949 50 national midget racing champions. Chuck Stevenson, Jack McGrath, Jimmy Davies and Gordon Reid also were slated to try their luck in Southern Illinois' largest annual sporting event.

Unfortunately, in the two years since the last Du Quoin race two more drivers had lost their lives along the championship trail. The great Rex Mays had been killed in November of 1949 during a race at Delmar, California. Walt Brown, another Du Quoin veteran, died in July of 1951 while racing in Pennsylvania. Besides Wallard, other drivers who had retired - whether forced to or by choice - included other former Du Quoin regulars Myron Fohr, Charlie Van Acker, Emil Andres, Mel Hansen and Eddie Zalucki.

After qualifications were completed, Johnnie Parsons, driving the Wynn's Friction Kurtis 3000, became the fastest man on the grid with a speed of 98.874 mph. On the outside of the first row was his old foe, Paul Russo, piloting a car he had constructed in the basement of his home with partner Ray Nichels. They had affectionately monikered the No. 7 machine "Basement Bessie."

Johnnie Parsons took the pole position with a speed of 98.87-mph for the first race of 1951. (The Phil Harms Collection)

Paul Russo qualified second in the home-built "Basement Bessie" and was the only other driver to exceed 98-mph. (The Phil Harms Collection)

That Magic Mile

Gordon Reid (73) ran strong until his gearbox shattered during lap 40. Here he rides almost standing in his race car on the inside line to allow Chuck Stevenson (8) and Sam Hanks (39) a clear track. (Photo by Bob Scott)

The car of Duane Carter (14) remained against the guardrail for the last 54 laps of the race after flipping in turn two. Joe Garson (77) and Bill Schindler (10) continue to race. (The Bruce Craig Collection)

Starting third was newcomer Jack McGrath in the Kurtis 4000, with Duane Carter next in fourth. Fifth was Andy Linden, also making his first appearance at Du Quoin, while defending Du Quoin champion, Bettenhausen, would start from sixth.

On the pace lap the field of 18 cars came down the front straightaway in even formation for the start. When the green flag fell Russo picked off the 1950 Indy 500 winner, Parsons, and was the first into turn one. Third and fourth were McGrath and Carter. Bettenhausen moved up a slot on the backstretch and at the close of one lap he was past Carter. Bettenhausen kept up the charge and by the end of lap three was breathing right down the back of leader Russo's neck. No longed equipped with the little super-charged midget powerplant that had taken No. 99 to victory in 1949, the larger Offenhauser motor now in Bettenhausen's car was proving to be stronger than the competition early on.

With just one more lap Bettenhausen had the lead and was never threatened for the remaining 96 laps. The real race took place for the second spot as Russo and Parsons battled back and forth. But the furious pace was interrupted on lap 40 when the gearbox of Gordon Reid's car decided to head south, slowing the remaining 17 cars as the eighth-place starter coasted back to the pits.

While Russo and Parsons continued to tangle, trouble was just around the corner for fifth-place Duane Carter. On lap 46 his car's right front tire blew out in the south turn and once again a horrified Du Quoin crowd fell silent as Carter's Ewing Offy rolled end-over-end. Carter rode it out and landed upright, still in the cockpit. The cars slowed drastically when a yellow caution flag was displayed. Carter was helped away from the wrecked machine in shock and with a bruised eye. His badly damaged car remained against the guardrail for the remainder of the race.

On the restart, Bettenhausen continued in his first place position and again began to stretch out to a comfortable lead. Russo seemed to be in firm control of second place, followed by Parsons, who had either backed-off or was down on power. Walt Faulkner had moved from seventh at the start and was now in fourth. Sam Hanks and Henry Banks comprised the fifth and sixth positions.

At the 80-mile mark, Parson's pit crew, who had agonized over tire wear and the fuel consumption of the thirsty Kurtis Kraft, finally gave their driver the OK signal to take Russo. And take Russo he did, passing him for good on lap 92 amid cheers from the grandstand.

Bettenhausen picked up another 200 points for the win, while Parsons collected 180. Russo was awarded 160 for third and AAA title contender Faulkner finished in fourth grabbing a much needed 140 points. In fifth was Sam Hanks, ending his first Du Quoin race with 120 points along with a swollen jaw – the result of a rock thrown up from the track surface by another car. In sixth was the 1950 national champion, Banks.

The tired drivers would rest. They would need to. Less than 48 hours later, Labor Day qualifications began earlier than usual at 11 a.m. Extra time was needed for the race, as it would be twice as long in distance than the regularly scheduled 100-mile event.

Again, 22-cars were rolled onto the track in front of the sold-out grandstand and the drivers climbed into the brightly colored machines to make their qualification runs. Tony Bettenhausen continued his domination of the field and posted a fast lap of 97.324, going almost a full mile an hour faster than the number two starter, Walt Faulkner. Faulkner was the driver with the best chance of catching Bettenhausen in the season's points battle. Not only was the pocket-sized Faulkner trailing Bettenhausen closely in points, but he was also the driver who had won the other two races of the season which were 200 and 250-miles in distance. Faulkner, of Long Beach, California, knew exactly how to pace himself and his car to go the distance.

Gordon Ried had repaired the gearbox of his McNamara Offy and would start in third. In fourth was Jimmy Davies driving the Parka-Pawl Special, which he had put into 13th place in his first race at Du Quoin on Saturday. Andy Linden, another driver who had fared well in his first

That Magic Mile

After winning Saturday's event, Tony Bettenhausen (99) started on the pole for Monday's race. Here he leads the field on the pace lap as Manuel Ayulo (31) waits to join the starting lineup. (The Bruce Craig Collection)

Walt Faulkner in the Agajanian Grant entry placed second in the Labor Day race and lost the points chase for the AAA's National Championship. (Photo by Bob Scott)

Tony Bettenhausen won both races of 1951 and became Du Quoin's first three-time winner. (Courtesy of the Indianapolis Motor Speedway)

race at Du Quoin finishing ninth, would start in fifth, just as he had two days before.

At the start Bettenhausen turned on the power and beat the field into the first turn and began setting a pace no other car could match. After five laps he held an advantage of almost a full straight-away, but on the next lap Jimmy Davies crashed into the guardrail in the second turn and the yellow caution flag appeared to slow the field. Davies was removed from his machine as the other cars rolled slowly by. Though he did not appear to be seriously injured, Davis was transported to Marshall Browning Hospital for X-rays.

On the restart it was again Bettenhausen's blue and gold No. 99 that took off, leaving the rest of the field in its dust. By lap 35 he began to overtake the field. But again there was trouble in turn two as Johnnie Parsons hit the guardrail and flipped his car. The yellow flag again flew to slow the field. Miraculously, the former Du Quoin winner was unhurt and walked away as the fans cheered.

That Magic Mile

Again the cars came up to speed and just as before it was all Tinley Park Tony's show. The Belanger roared around and around the track as it picked off car after car. The rest of the field could do nothing but hold on and hope that the No. 99 car would break down. Not a chance. The Belanger was too well-prepared for the 200-miler and was leading handily until lap 93 when raindrops began to fall.

The yellow flag came out and the cars slowed to run in position for eight more laps under caution. AAA rules dictated that an event had to be run at least past the halfway point to count towards the championship; so, at the end of lap 101, the red flag appeared and the race was halted. The track surface had become too slippery and dangerous for racing.

Bettenhausen, who completed the race a full three laps ahead of the rest of the field, won his fifth race of the year and his third in a row at Du Quoin to collect 202 points for the win. Title contender Faulkner was second and was awarded 161.6 points for his finish. Bettenhausen won three more races in 1951 and became the AAA big car champion for the first time in his career. Faulkner finished high enough in the remaining races to end the season in third place in the standings behind Henry Banks, who ended the season second in the points despite not winning a single race that year.

Sam Hanks, who started in 10th in his second race at Du Quoin, managed a third place finish in the race, while Chuck Stevenson came in a respectable fourth. Banks was fifth.

"No Women Allowed"
September 1, 1952

Twenty-eight cars were transported to Southern Illinois for the sixth running of the Ted Horn Memorial. Five of the year's top-10 Indy finishers had made the trip. They included runner up Jim Rathmann, making his first appearance; third place Sam Hanks; Jimmy Reece (seventh); George Connor (eighth) and Cliff Griffith, who finished ninth in the 500.

Conspicuous due to his absence was Tony Bettenhausen. On June 8, a week after his disheartening 24th place finish at Indy, he failed to qualify in the No. 99 Belanger on the mile oval at Milwaukee. His friend and fellow racer, Johnny McDowell, was also killed that afternoon at the same track. Bettenhausen had lost more than 20 friends and competitors in racing accidents since his career as a professional driver blossomed after World War II. He announced his retirement from dirt track racing and claimed that he would only drive in the Indianapolis 500 from then on. In six starts at the speedway, he had never finished better than ninth.

Another missing driver, whose absence drew attention from the 10,542 fans surrounding the guardrail-enclosed track, was the year's Indianapolis 500 winner, Troy Ruttman.

Ruttman, a former California hot-rodder who had won both the AAA's Midwest and West Coast sprint car championships in 1951, had been recruited by J.C. Agajanian to drive his car again at Indy for the second year in a row. Agajanian, a long time car owner, auto-racing promoter and all around benefactor of the sport, had an eye for talent. Not only was Agajanian a good judge of the drivers that he chose to pilot his racing cars, but also in the mechanical talent he selected to work on them. The California pork baron entered Ruttman in one of his cars that was prepared by the renowned mechanic Clay Smith. Agajanian was rewarded when Ruttman battled Bill Vukovich for the lead lap-after-lap, until a steering pin sheered in then leader Vukovich's Fuel Injection Special, sending the "Mad Russian" into the second turn wall. At 22

Bill Schindler took the pole in 1952 with a speed of 92.17 mph. (The Phil Harms Collection)

years of age, the big blond Ruttman led the last nine laps to become the youngset winner ever in the history of the speedway. The same year, he won the inuagural 200-mile pavement track race at Raleigh, N.C., and gained a massive lead of 1,410 points in the AAA's big car standings after only three races in 1952. But Ruttman, also committed to the West Coast sprint car championship that year, suffered serious injuries while campaigning one of the smaller cars at Cedar Rapids, Iowa, two weeks prior to Du Quoin. This forced him to sit out the rest of the season. However, Ruttman still won the sprint championship that year, despite not driving in another race.

*Schindler, driving "Basement Bessie" leads the pack to the green flag.
(The Phil Harms Collection)*

*Henry Banks in the No.2 Blue Crown Spark Plug Special brings up the rear.
(Courtesy of WDQN Radio)*

Du Quoin rookie, Bob Sweikert (22), Jimmy Reece (44) and the "Mad Russian," Bill Vukovich (98) do battle during the early laps. Vukovich would eventually finish the race in third place driving the car of the injured Indianapolis 500 winner, Troy Ruttman. (The Phil Harms Collection)

That Magic Mile

With six races of the year over, another California driver, Chuck Stevenson of Fresno, was the closest challenger Ruttman had for the title. With only one victory that year - posted in the second race held at Milwaukee in August - Stevenson had built up 885 points, but was still a long way behind the Indy winner. Stevenson had finished 18th at Indy, seventh in the "Rex Mays Classic" in June at Milwaukee, sixth on the pavement at Raleigh, fifth in Springfield and was third at Detroit. The consistent Stevenson still had a chance to catch Ruttman for the championship. But it was a slim one. He would have to finish in fourth place or better in the season's five remaining 100-mile grinds.

Stevenson had been piloting the Springfield Welding car owned and entered by Bessie Lee Paoli, a prominent resident of the Illinois capital. Paoli was not the first women to own a racing car, but she was the first to own one with the capability of taking its driver to a big car title. Of course this created a problem because of the AAA's strictly enforced rule that prohibited women from entry into the pit areas at the race tracks. There was absolutely no exception to this rule, unless a nurse was required for an injury. As a result, race after race (even in front of the hometown crowd at Springfield) Paoli had to assume the role of spectator at events in which she was officially entered as a participant. It would have been interesting to hear what the lovely Bessie Lee had to say about such a ridiculous situation.

Other drivers at Du Quoin included Bill Schindler, the winner of the year's Springfield race, back for his second time around the oval. He was driving Basement Bessie, which he had purchased from Paul Russo during the winter. He had taken the home-built racing car to a 16th place finish at Indianapolis. Russo, for the second time at Du Quoin, was to fill the vacated cockpit of the Belanger for Bettenhausen. This time the No. 99 ride might turn into a permanent one for the always competitive Russo.

Sam Hanks would drive the Bardahl Special in his fourth start in Southern Illinois. By a strange twist of fate, Bill Vukovich in his second start occupied the seat of Indy rival Ruttman's winning car. Since his regular driver couldn't make the race, J.C. Agajanian obviously felt it prudent to employ the driver who almost spoiled his first victory as a car owner at Indianapolis.

Also entered was rising star Bob Sweikert, a rookie at Du Quoin. Jack McGrath would drive the Hinkle Special in his third appearance on the fairground's track. Jimmy Reece was in the John Zink entry and Ebe Yoder would make his debut behind the wheel of the City of Goshen entry owned by retired driver, Charlie Van Acker.

As time trials began rain threatened to spoil the Labor Day holiday. The humidity hung thick in the air, and would surely slow down the cars due to the effect the moisture would have on the engines. At the close of the qualification session, Bill Schindler, who had lost his left leg after a racing accident in 1936, laid down the fastest time with a 39.06 clocking of 92.166 mph. A speed that was well-below the record run of better than 100-mph set by Bettenhausen in 1949. The slowest qualifier of the day was rookie Chuck Weyant. With his speed of 88.75 mph, it made the 1952 field of 18 cars the slowest yet on the usually fast Du Quoin track.

When the race began, Schindler made good on his pole position and led the pack for the first 27 laps. But the frontman suffered the same engine hex as race leaders before him and his car's power faded badly, causing him to run at the rear of the pack. The Hinkle driver, Jack McGrath, who had started fourth, inherited the lead and began to enjoy his best performance yet at Du Quoin. He liked leading the race so much that he pushed his car harder and harder to build on his already substantial lead. But his car's right-rear Firestone tire would have none of it and wore out quickly, forcing McGrath to surrender his lead on the 68th lick as he entered the pits for fresh rubber.

Title contender Chuck Stevenson was right there. He had started in sixth and one by one he had picked his way through the leading group of cars up to second place. Thirty-two laps remained. If Stevenson could hold on for the win he would boost his point total to 1,085. With four more races to go after this one he would be in striking distance of Ruttman, who could gain nothing toward the championship from his hospital bed.

Stevenson maintained his lead and won the race. The pace was slowed only once when former front-runner Schindler - trying hard to make up the two laps he lost because of his pit stop - spun out in the first turn on lap 97, causing the only dangerous incident of the day. The cars drove the last three miles under the caution flag.

Hanks held off Vukovich for second, while Russo was there at the finish to claim fourth. Mid-race leader McGrath did come back from his two lap-deficit to round out the top five, recording his best showing at Du Quoin.

It was a happy Bessie Lee Paoli who cheered from the grandstand as her Springfield Welding car crossed the finish line in first place. Not only did her car win the race, but Stevenson went on to place well enough in the season's remaining races to clinch the driver's championship, beating out Ruttman by just 30 points. Bessie Lee may never have made it into the pits at the races, but she was a guest of honor at that year's annual AAA awards banquet.

Chuck Stevenson and car owner, Bessie Lee Paoli, pose with the winner's trophy. (The Phil Harms Collection)

That Magic Mile

The Thin Man
September 7, 1953

William R. Hayes succumbed to a heart attack ten days after the 1952 Labor Day race at the fairgrounds he had created three decades earlier. Many were saddened and affected by the news of his passing.

Operation of the fairground and the numerous other Hayes' family holdings were passed on to his two sons, Gene and Don, who believed that the fair should serve as a tribute to their father's memory. In the tradition of their father, the two brothers committed themselves to provide the best entertainment possible for the people of Southern Illinois. As a result, during the next few years the motorsports program held on the fair's dirt oval was expanded. The already existing motorcycle and midget car races would continue and by 1954 the fair would also schedule both sprint car and stock car races. But the fair's racing card was always highlighted by the running of the big cars on Labor Day.

Joe E. "Buck" Kidd was retained as the promotor of the Ted Horn Memorial and for the 1953 race a record 32 cars and drivers entered. On top of that, Kidd boasted a record purse of more than $15,000 to be split between the 18 drivers who would qualify for the seventh running of the AAA chariot race, with almost $4,000 going to the winner.

A new crop of drivers was emerging in the top ranks of the sport and many of them hailed from the West Coast and Southwestern portion of the United States. When the 12 race national championship season began at Indianapolis in May, many racing cars could be seen being transported east on Route 66 to begin competing for the driver's title. Even though racing was a flourishing sport out West the drivers knew that they had to go in the opposite direction to compete for the national crown. Ten of the 12 scheduled championship events in 1953 were held east of the Mississippi. At least a third of the field entered at Du Quoin for the 1953 race hailed from California.

The winner of Du Quoin's 1953 midget car race, Mike Nazaruk, looked to double-up in victory lane after capturing the pole position for the big car event. (The Phil Harms Collection)

These drivers included Du Quoin's defending champion, Chuck Stevenson, who had signed as driver for J.C. Agajanian, owner of the Kuzma Offenhauser car that was wrenched by Clay Smith. An Indianapolis 500 winning mechanic, Smith also had tuned cars toward an Indianapolis 500 pole position, two Indy qualifying records and was responsible for the preparation of the last car to complete the 500-miler without a single pit stop. Most recently, he had prepared a winning car for Stevenson for the 200-mile race at Milwaukee just a week before.

A view of the pit area prior to the 1953 Ted Horn Memorial. (The Phil Harms Collection)

That Magic Mile

From left to right, Tony Bettenhausen (99), Mike Nazaruk (73) and Chuck Weyant (35) mix it up early in the race. Bettenhausen led the first 70 laps of the event. (The Phil Harms Collection)

Sam Hanks, who finished third in the Indianapolis 500, was piloting the Bardahl Special and was returning for his fifth trip around Du Quoin's mile.

Hanks was in possession of an impressive Illinois driving record. In his four starts at Du Quoin, he had finished fifth in the first race of 1951 and third in the second contest that year. A year before he landed in second. At Springfield his record was even more impressive. In his first appearance there in 1952 he wound up in third, was second in the first of two races in 1953 and won the latter 100-miler to nail down his first Indy car championship trophy. Returning to racing after World War II, where he had served for almost four years, rising to the rank of First Lieutenant, Hanks was tabbed as the "long, tall racing gentleman." The six foot, 165-pound Hanks was a fierce competitor and often drove despite injury.

Jack McGrath also was back. He had won the second big car race of his career at the Milwaukee 100 in June; and, as a result, was locked in a battle for the driving title with a slim 21-point lead over Hanks. McGrath had led for 41 laps in the 1952 Du Quoin race.

Bill Vukovich, the winner of the 1953 Indianapolis 500, had not faired well in the other five races leading up to Du Quoin, but was not to be discounted. The year's 500 had been one of the toughest ever due to the blistering track temperature of over 130 degrees. Every driver suffered from the effects of heat exhaustion and even one driver, Carl Scarborough, had died as a result. Only eight of the original 33 starting drivers finished the race. Some asked for relief from the drivers who were already sidelined, but Vukovich soldiered on, aided by dousings of cool water while his crew performed the three scheduled pit stops on his Kurtis KK500A. Vukovich would lead all but five laps of the grueling race.

Roger Ward, the former P-38 fighter pilot, who had so far won two races in 1953 could not be ignored. He had been victorious at the June Springfield race and had won the shortened 51-lap grind at Detroit on the 4th of July.

Sam Hanks made a 43-second pit stop for two tires on lap 83 and took the 1953 race for his first win in Southern Illinois. (Courtesy of the Indianapolis Motor Speedway)

The return of Tony Bettenhausen also would be a factor. He had come out of retirement a week before to serve as relief driver at the Milwaukee event. For the Du Quoin race he would coach his old No. 99 Belanger around a very familiar stomping ground. The car sported new yellow, blue and gold colors and letterings for its sponsor, Miracle Power, and many fans and fellow competitors were aware that Tony could recreate the dominance that he showed in the races at Du Quoin in 1949 and 1951.

At high noon, qualifying commenced and Johnnie Parsons was the first out on the track piloting the Equa Flow Exhaust car, setting a speed of 92.807 mph. But a few minutes later, one of the few East Coast drivers in the qualifying order, Mike Nazaruk, of Long Island, New York, set the pace with his fast lap of 93.750. Within the hour, Nazaruk's time of 38.40 was still standing and the pole was his. Nazaruk had won the midget car race at Du Quoin two days before. Behind the wheel of the McNamara Special, Nazaruk, a real favorite with the fans, happily faced the possibility of following up his midget victory with a win in the big cars.

Starting behind Nazaruk was Californian Don Freeland driving the Bob Estes entered Watson Offenhauser. Freeland, who was campaigning in his rookie year in the champ cars, qualified just .20 of a second slower than Nazaruk. "Big Don," as he was known, had won the pole in his first race at Springfield and had brought his car home to a respectable third place finish. In his second appearance on the state capital's mile he had started 11th and wound up in seventh.

Third on the grid was Hanks, followed by Cal Niday, another Californian also enjoying a remarkable rookie season. He was offered a drive in the Belanger car in May at Indianapolis, but finished 30th after being sidelined with electrical problems. Niday also had two top ten finishes at Springfield in June and August. Starting in fifth was the previous year's winner, Chuck Stevenson.

When the race started it seemed like 1951 all over again as Bettenhausen shot from the third row into first place to lead the field. Meanwhile, Hanks got by Freeland into third place while Nazaruk maintained second. Jack McGrath, who had started eighth in the Hinkle car, was on the charge and was picking off cars fast enough to get into second place by lap 13. Hanks and Parsons started dicing for third and it wasn't until mid-race that Hanks found himself pressuring McGrath for second behind runaway race leader, Bettenhausen.

Pit stops began near the 60th lap when Stevenson headed in for fresh tires. Bettenhausen stayed in the lead, trying to outlast McGrath, but after ten more laps the Belanger rolled in and McGrath took over the lead. Hanks, now in second, also remained on the track. The two drivers played a waiting game to see who would pit first. Finally, on the 83rd tour, it was Hanks who checked in for a quick 43 second servicing.

Bettenhausen, quickly back out on the track was making up time; but, unbeknownst to the Tinley Park ace, gear fluid was leaking from his car and by lap 85 his car's gearbox fried. Bettenhausen would become the only driver who would fail to finish the race because of a mechanical problem.

McGrath had almost a full mile lead on Hanks and kept it for the next eight laps; but, just as in 1952, McGrath's right-rear Firestone failed him. The tire blew and sent the brave Irishman's car heading toward the guardrail. McGrath kept his machine out of harm's way and nursed the Hinkle to his pit, hoping to get back into the action to at least collect a few points for his trouble.

But it was Hank's race. The "Thin Man," shot away from the field with four laps to go and finished the race almost a full mile ahead of the competition. Hanks also set a new Du Quoin clocking with an average race speed of 89.984 mph, breaking Chuck Stevenson's 1952 record speed of 88.409.

Manuel Ayulo, who had started in ninth place drove a conservative and trouble-free race coasted home to a second place finish for his best showing in three races at Du Quoin. Third was Johnnie Parsons, who had begun the day in 11th place. McGrath salvaged fourth place, which was good enough to keep his points lead over Hanks alive by a slim margin. However, Hanks would eventually clinch the AAA title, beating McGrath by more than 400 points at season's end.

Tony Bettenhausen was listed as last, but had served notice that he was back, winning two of the four remaining championship races held in 1953.

Winning Ugly
September 6, 1954

Changes were taking place on the American auto racing scene during the first half of the decade between 1950 and 1960 that would eventually alter the complexion of the National Championship series.

The one-mile Milwaukee dirt track was paved with asphalt and completed in time for the first of its two races in 1954. Along with the addition of an event on the already paved Darlington, South Carolina track, and the annual running of the Indianapolis 500, four races out of the expanded 13-race 1954 schedule would be run on pavement tracks. Another change that occured in 1952 was shifting the big car series in another costly direction.

That year California race car builder Frank Kurtis introduced a newly designed racing car that would become known as the "roadster." This type of car utilized a drive shaft that ran next to the driver instead of directly beneath the cockpit of the car. Also, Kurtis found that by tilting the four cylinder Offenhauser engine - used by almost every competitor - he created a shorter and wider car with a lower center of gravity that allowed the car to travel through the turns of a paved track almost 15- miles an hour faster than the more traditional racing cars.

Bill Vukovich won both the 1953 and 1954 Indianapolis 500's in the Kurtis designed roadster, while the other races held on both the dirt and pavement tracks were won by drivers in conventional dirt cars.

The writing was on the wall. Eventually, car owners would have to purchase two different types of cars to campaign the entire season. Even more important was the fact that they would need to hire drivers who would be competitive on both dirt and pavement.

But in 1954 it was still possible to see the best of both worlds on the same track. Such was the case with drivers Chuck Stevenson and Manuel Ayulo

A determined Don Freeland swept the pole from Sam Hanks with a speed of 97.50 mph and led the first 73 laps of the 1954 Ted Horn Memorial. (The Phil Harms Collection)

Both drivers still piloted the conventional dirt cars, and were able to park them in victory lane at both Milwaukee and Darlington. Stevenson won the 100-mile race at Milwaukee after finishing 12th in the Indianapolis 500 the week before. Ayulo finished 13th in the 500 and won 200-mile events in June at Darlington and in August at Milwaukee, a week prior to the annual race at Du Quoin.

On the dirt tracks, two drivers posted their first National Championship wins. Jimmy Bryan, a rising star from Phoenix, Arizona, who had finished second in the 1954 Indianapolis 500, won the 100-mile race at Langhorne, Pennsylvania, while Jimmy Davies finally won the Springfield race after five frustrating attempts.

That Magic Mile

Don Freeland (7) leads Jimmy Bryan (9), Sam Hanks (99) and the rest of the field just after the start. (The Phil Harms Collection)

Roger Ward started 15th in the Central Excavating Special and worked his way up to run with the frontrunners before his out-of-control car caused the death of mechanic, Clay Smith. (The Phil Harms Collection)

That Magic Mile

Ward's upside down car is parked against the guardrail where it came to rest as Clay Smith's body is about to be loaded into the automobile at the left.

Accident victims receive attention from AAA officials and volunteers. (Photos courtesy of the Du Quoin State Fair)

The cigar chomping Bryan, who stood well over six feet tall, also would win the last four dirt races held in 1954 at the Indiana State Fairgrounds, at Sacramento, Phoenix and Las Vegas. Known as the "Phoenix Cowboy," Bryan's rise in the sport of automobile racing was phenomenal. He would clinch the National Championship in 1954, beating Ayulo by well over 1300 points.

The 1954 race weekend at Du Quoin started off with a stock car race and then the sprint cars took to the oval for their show. When the time came on Monday for the big cars to qualify, West Coast midget veteran Andy Linden pushed all of his 200-pound frame into his right foot and put old reliable Basement Bessie into the top spot with a speed of 95.01 mph. Then it was defending champion Hanks - now piloting the No. 99 Belanger - who secured the number one starting position with his lap of 96.36. But Don Freeland, the other big guy from the West Coast, would have none of it and went out and turned the Southern Illinois saucer more than a mile an hour faster in the Bob Estes entry, pulling the rug right out from under Hanks.

When all 36 cars had finished their time trials, Freeland, Hanks, Linden, DuQuoin rookie Ray Crawford, Nazaruk, Davies, Parsons (driving the Bardahl car he had wrecked here in 1951), Bryan, Duane Carter and Bob Sweikert made up the top-ten drivers of the 18 that would start the race.

Surprisingly, the "Peruvian Spark Plug," Ayulo, failed to qualify at Du Quoin. With five 100-mile races left in the season, this situation would greatly enhance Bryan's 660-point cushion in the chase for the driver's title.

When Bill Vandewater dropped the green flag, Freeland shot into the first turn, but hard charging Bryan came from his eighth place starting spot to challenge "Big Don" before the end of the first lap. Freeland held firm and began to build on his pole position start, stretching out his advantage to almost half a mile. Meanwhile, Hanks kept pressure on Bryan to regain second, and within a few laps he did. Freeland still led at lap 25 and a win at Du Quoin looked to be in the bag for the popular California driver.

Master Indy car mechanic, Clay Smith, was the last fatality in National Championship racing on the Du Quoin mile.
(The Phil Harms Collection)

The 1952 winner, Chuck Stevenson, who began the race in 13th, was making time and was up with the front pack, running behind Davies and Linden. Crawford had drifted to the rear, while Carter was already out of the action and parked in the pits.

Sam Hanks collected a shallow victory with his second win in Southern Illinois. (The Phil Harms Collection)

At lap 30 Hanks began to catch up to Freeland, while Davies took third from Bryan. On lap 37, Freeland entered the pits for what the 14,700 fans assumed to be an early tire change, but Freeland was out of his car and obviously in a rage. He was finished for the day. A faulty magneto had cost him the race.

Hanks now possessed the lead. Crawford dropped out of his first race at Du Quoin. Davies came off the fourth turn and dove into the pits for fresh tires while Stevenson and Bryan remained on the track in hot pursuit of the "Thin Man."

At lap 81 Hanks remained firmly in command and back-to-back wins were in the cards, but fate dealt an especially cruel hand on the next lap. Roger Ward, who had started the race in 15th, had steadily moved up to run with the top five cars. He was about to be lapped by Stevenson when the two cars came together at the start of the front straightaway. Stevenson kept his car under control, but Ward could not rein in his No. 81 Central Excavating Special and the car slid down the main straightaway rear end first. It then began a series of rolls heading right toward the pit area where many crew members were out on the track with their driver's signal boards. The horrified fans fell silent as Stevenson's mechanic, Clay Smith, was struck by Ward's car, killing him instantly. Eight others in the pit area were injured, including two children. Ward escaped serious injury.

Jessie Feldscher, then a 22-year-old resident of Elkville, Illinois, located just south of Du Quoin, recalls the accident, "I snuck into the pit area of my favorite driver, Jimmy Bryan. I was standing with my foot up on the guardrail when I saw Stevenson and Ward come together. All I could think to do was run, and run I did when I saw Ward's car coming at me. At the time I didn't know it, but one of the tires that came off of Ward's car hit me in the back, knocked me out and sent me flying through the air. When I came to, Hanks was standing over me. I tried to get up because I was lying on my camera and I remember he told me not to worry about that. 'You might have a broken back,' he said. I was laid up for over three months." Feldscher, despite the horror of the accident, remained a passionate racing fan and went on to attend many more Du Quoin races and 41 consecutive Indianapolis 500's.

After the accident the race ran for two laps under the yellow and was finally red flagged, with Hanks being officially listed as the winner and taking home $3,500 of the $14,000 purse. There was no ceremony in victory lane that year. The winner's trophy was silently deposited in the cockpit of Hank's car.

Stevenson, listed as second, was so affected by the death of Smith, his friend and mechanic, that he retired from racing right then and there. Bryan was credited with third, which added another 140 points in his bid for the championship. He was followed by Jimmy Davies and Jimmy Reece, who had started 17th.

That Magic Mile

The Pits
September 5, 1955

Indeed, the 1954 season ended on a sad note, but 1955 would be the most tragic year to date for not only the National Championship series, but for auto racing around the world.

In Europe, where many automobile races were still run on temporarily closed public highways, several spectators, including a small child, were killed during the 1,000-mile-long Mille Miglia road race held on the roads of Northern and Central Italy on the first weekend of May.

Six American drivers, including three veteran big car pilots, would loose their lives before the ninth running of the Du Quoin race on Labor Day. Mike Nazaruk would die during a race at Langhorne on May 1. Manuel Ayulo would be fatally injured on May 16 at the Indianapolis Motor Speedway after crashing into the southwest wall during practice. On May 30, while leading the 500 and possibly on his way to a third consecutive victory, Bill Vukovich died in a flaming crash during the 57th lap of the race. It happened after a four car accident on the backstretch that was triggered by an out of control car.

But the worst was yet to come. The world's most celebrated sports car race, the 24-hours of Le Mans, held annually in France since 1906, became the site of racing's bloodiest carnage on June 11.

On Le Mans' half mile long main straightaway, a Mercedes Benz, flying along at a speed of over 160 mph, went out of control after colliding with another car, a British Austin Healy. The German racing car plowed into a retaining wall, disintigrating into flaming metal fragments that flew like shrapnel into the crowd, killing and maiming. Two children were decapitated, as was the driver of the Mercedes, whose body was burned beyond recognition. The British car did much of the same, but the driver managed to escape with his life. A total of 82 spectators died, while more than 100 others were injured. Unbelievably, the race was continued.

44

Eddie Russo surprised the field with a qualifying run of 98.47 mph in the Sumar Blough entry going a mile-an-hour faster than Don Freeland had in 1954. It was Russo's first and only National Championship pole. (The Phil Harms Collection)

Automobile racing was temporarily banned for a time in many European countries. In Switzerland it was stopped permanently. Racing was also halted in Mexico, where the 1,000-mile long Pan American road race had been run since 1951.

With his win at Du Quoin, Jimmy Bryan broke Tony Bettenhausen's 100-lap record of 90.065 mph set in 1949. It was also Bryan's seventh win in a row on a dirt track and his eighth consecutive 100-mile victory. (The Phil Harms Collection)

In the United States the Hearst newspaper chain - a longtime anti-racing protagonist - cried for an end to what it called "bloodsport," and compared it to chariot racing during the decline of the Roman Empire.

Eventually, the American Automobile Association - which had controlled racing in the United States since 1902 - would succumb to the pressure. On August 3 it announced from Washington D.C., that it would no longer sanction races after the close of the 1955 season.

The negative publicity and anti-racing fervor also affected the Du Quoin race. This was evident when just over 9,000 fans paid for their grandstand tickets at the fairground. But it didn't diminish the drivers' desire to compete, and 33 cars appeared to qualify for the race.

Defending champion Sam Hanks was not among the drivers. He, like others before him, had decided to concentrate on winning the Indianapolis 500. After 11 races on the massive oval, the trip to victory lane still eluded the talented driver.

That Magic Mile

The 1955 Indianapolis 500 winner, Bob Sweikert, enjoyed a well deserved cold-one after a fourth-place finish at Du Quoin netted him the AAA National Championship. (Photo by Gene Gallmeister)

But the winner of the 500, Bob Sweikert, was at Du Quoin and ready to maintain his more than 1,200 point margin in the chase for the National Championship. Sweikert was tough and the competition knew it. And, he was piloting the John Zink Special maintained by A.J. Watson, one of Indy car racing's all-time winningest mechanics. His nearest rival, Johnny Thomson, a highly decorated war hero and the 1954 Eastern Sprint Car champion, had been badly injured during the Langhorne race and was still healing.

Every race during the 1955 season was a gigantic struggle between Sweikert and Jimmy Bryan. The Cowboy didn't even care about racking up points. Pure and simple, he was out to win every race. With his August 20 victory at Springfield, he had become the first driver in the history of the National Championship to win six consecutive races on dirt tracks.

Surprisingly, after time trials were completed, neither Sweikert or Bryan was able to secure the inside front row starting position, nor did former polesitter, Freeland; or Jack McGrath, Andy Linden or Jimmy Davies. All former Du Quoin hot shoes.

Tony Bettenhausen and Johnnie Parsons, both former winners, didn't even make the cut. Duane Carter and Ward would not start the race either.

Instead, the honor of the pole position went to Eddie Russo. It was the young driver's second start in Southern Illinois. He had finished in 15th place in the 1953 event, right behind his Uncle Paul. The older Russo - like Sam Hanks - now focused all of his energy on achieving victory at Indianapolis.

The order behind Russo's top qualifying spot was Linden, Sweikert and Du Quoin rookies, Eddie Johnson and George Amick. Then came Freeland, while three more first-time Du Quoin starters, Shorty Templeman, Jimmy Daywalt and Pat O'Connor completed the top ten.

Bryan would begin the 100-miler in 12th, with other notables McGrath and Davies starting 15th and 17th respectively. Buddy Cagle, making his first ever big car appearance, would be 18th and last on the grid.

After the unusually lengthy invocation, Johnnie Parsons found himself at the wheel of the pace car guiding the field around for the parade lap. His passengers included Judge George Ober, who had been requested by the Indianapolis Motor Speedway owner, Tony Hulman, to chair the committee that would craft the still unnamed organization that would fill the void left by the departing AAA.

As the fans cheered, the starting flag dropped and Russo moved to the outside groove and headed the field into the first turn. Sweikert moved past Linden's Kuzma Offy and on the fifth lap the John Zink pilot disposed of Russo's blue and white No. 48.

Quickly, Freeland moved into third driving the No. 12 Bob Estes entry, but Bryan had shot from 12th and was already applying pressure to the tail of Big Don's car.

By the 41st lap, Bryan had passed Freeland, who was slowing to enter the pits. For the second year in a row he failed to finish the race. With fuel leaking from his car, Freeland made the prudent move and parked his car as close as possible to one of the many fire crews stationed around the track.

Soon after the crossed flags were displayed signaling the halfway point of the race, pit stops began. Jimmy Davies was the first in for service, but Sweikert and Bryan remained on the track. Sweikert fell back in an attempt to conserve rubber, and on lap 79 Linden moved into the lead. Now the order behind the leader was Sweikert, Bryan, McGrath and Amick, one of the year's Du Quoin rookies.

By lap 81, Linden, who had choosen not to pit, finally headed in for a tire change. He must have sensed that the leaders - none of which had yet made a stop - would find trouble in the closing laps. Sweikert was again in the lead.

Bryan began to pressure Sweikert during the last ten laps, and the white warning belt under the rubber on the John Zink car's right rear tire began to show. But, Sweikert threw caution to the wind and pushed his throttle almost through the floorboard getting all he could from the car as the white flag flew for the last lap.

Sweikert made it into the second turn just as his tire let go, sending him into the guardrail. He was able to keep the car upright and escape injury while Bryan flew by with McGrath and Amick right behind.

After six consecutive starts on the Magic Mile, Jack McGrath finally managed a second place showing in 1955. (The Phil Harms Collection)

The Cowboy posted his eighth straight 100-mile victory in a row - his seventh on a dirt track - and with a race free of yellow flags, broke the race record set by Bettenhausen (90.065 mph) in 1949 with his speed of 93.530 mph.

The race was stopped because Sweikert's car created a hazard for the remainder of the field, who were all at least one-lap down. This gave Sweikert a fourth place finish and 140 points, which was good enough to clinch the last ever AAA National Championship. By the end of the season, Sweikert, on the strength of the 1,000 points from his victory at the 500, would accumulate 2,290 points, compared to Bryan's 1,480.

Before another year was over, Du Quoin veterans Sweikert, McGrath and Walt Faulkner would all die in racing accidents.

That Magic Mile

Back In The Saddle
September 3, 1956

On January 1, 1956, National Championship racing passed into a new era. The United States Auto Club (USAC), which had been formulated in September the year before, began its commitment to the sport of automobile racing and undertook the sanctioning of almost all racing events in the country. All national championship big cars (including the Indianapolis 500 roadsters), sprints, midgets, the Pikes Peak hill climbers and a large portion of the ever growing stock cars raced under USAC rules. It was a noble experiment in organization, and had it not been for the still budding National Association of Stock Car Auto Racing (NASCAR) - which was formed in 1949 - the Indianapolis-based USAC may have controlled the sport completely.

Car owners, drivers, promoters and mechanics had sought and were given the opportunity to rule and govern themselves. Many of the old AAA supervisors and safety officials had made the transition to the new "club." Thomas W. Binford was named President of the new organization, and former national championship competitor, Duane Carter, hung up his helmet to become its first Director of Competition.

The first of the USAC's 12 races in the 1956 season was the Indianapolis 500. An almost unknown driver named Pat Flaherty won the event. He had taken over the John Zink car in the place of Sweikert, and had proved his ability by taking down both the pole and the race with record speeds.

By the time the championship trail had wound its way to Du Quoin on September 3, Flaherty had won again on the paved Milwaukee mile, ten days after the 500, but was critically injured during the Springfield race. He was out for the remainder of the season.

The next race - held on the dirt at Langhorne - was won by George Amick, driving Roger Ward's old Central Excavating Special, while Pat

The only driver to qualify at over 99 mph, pole man Johnny Thomson, led the first 42 laps of the 1956 Ted Horn Memorial.
(Courtesy of the Indianapolis Motor Speedway)

O'Connor was victorious on the Darlington pavement in the Sumar Blough. Back on the dirt in the inaugural race at Lakewood Park, near Atlanta, Eddie Sachs recorded his first win piloting the Glessner Special, formerly driven by midget car ace Shorty Templeman. In August, Jimmy Bryan returned to his old form and recorded back-to-back wins at Springfield. At the Milwaukee mile's second race of the season a week later, it was again Bryan in command of the field. Don Freeland, who had finished third at Indy, had placed well enough during the early part of the season to sit second in the points standings. But arriving at Du Quoin, Bryan, with his total of 1,000 markers, had come within 60 points of Freeland. First place, still held by the mending Flaherty with 1,500 points, was also under threat with five 100-mile races remaining. Each race would award 200 points to the winner.

That Magic Mile

Johnny Thomson (45) hit a rut in the marbles as Jimmy Bryan (2) slid by to take the lead. (The Phil Harms Collection)

Buck Kidd, who had continually supplied Du Quoin fans with nothing less than an always exciting program, was still retained as promotor of the event by the Hayes family, with no objection from the USAC. With a purse of $14,626 up for grabs, racing returned to the fairground with renewed vigor. More than 16,000 fans packed the grandstand and surrounded the track.

Returning to Southern Illinois' magic mile was Tony Bettenhausen, who headed the list of 32 entries. Freeland was back, as was Amick, Andy Linden, Jimmy Davies, Bob Veith, Johnnie Boyd, Jimmy Daywalt, Ward, O'Connor and Parsons.

Du Quoin newcomers included rising star, Sachs, Jim Rathman, Jack Turner, Elmer George, Ed Elisian, Earl Motter, Charlie Musselman, Johnny Thomson and Don Branson.

When all of the cars and drivers had completed their individual two-lap dashes to determine the starting grid, Johnny Thomson, the "Flying Scot," held the pole with a record time of 36.14, for a speed of 99.613 mph. Second went to Freeland, who always seemed to make his mark at Du Quoin during qualifications. In 1955, he had been the sixth fastest starter, the polesitter in 1954, and second in 1953. To be sure, if Big Don could last the race he would be a force to be reckoned with.

That Magic Mile

Third on the grid was Branson, of Urbana, Illinois, a former aviation engineer who began racing midgets in 1946. Sitting fourth was Bettenhausen, followed by Bryan, Amick, Davies, George, Turner and Rathman.

Prominently heading the non-qualifier's list for the second year in a row were both Parsons and Ward, while Sachs, O'Connor, Easton and Van Johnson (no relation to the popular movie star), also failed to make the grade.

At the drop of the flag, Thomson, in the D-A Lubricants Special, charged fast, with Freeland - again in the Bob Estes entry - and Bettenhausen in the Schmidt Special, close behind. Next came Amick, Branson and Bryan.

On the fifth lap, Bryan swung by Branson's No. 74 Hoover Motors car and Amick's No. 81.

Bettenhausen soon disposed of Freeland, and on the 14th tour the Cowboy also moved past Big Don for third. Davies, in the Morcroft Special, was sidelined on the the 21st lap with engine failure and was the first to drop out. Two laps later, Bryan took control of second and could smell first place blood.

Ten laps later he tasted it, when Thomson, who had opened up a comfortable lead, hit a rut up in the outside groove and momentarily lost control of his No. 45. By the time the Scot had it back under control he was relegated to fifth place, while Bryan was past him and flying.

Meanwhile, Bettenhausen and Freeland dueled for second. Back and forth it went until lap 62, when Big Don dropped out for the second straight year with leaking fuel. Adding insult to injury, Freeland was instantly knocked out of second place in the points chase.

Thomson quickly regained his composure and was back up near the front and closing on Bettenhausen, making short work of the Tinley Park Express.

50

With his second consecutive Ted Horn Memorial victory, Jimmy Bryan went on to win the inaugural USAC National Championship. (Courtesy of the Indianapolis Motor Speedway)

As Bettenhausen faded to mid-pack, the order became Bryan, Thomson, Rathmann, Veith, and Amick, and, that's the way it remained until the checkered waved.

Bryan became the third driver to record back-to-back wins at Du Quoin. With 200 points for the victory he was now only 300 behind Flaherty. Never threatened during the rest of the season, the Cowboy rode roughshod over the competition. He came in second in the next race at Syracuse, N.Y., and collected another 160 points. He won again at the Indiana State Fair (200 points), and took third at Sacramento (140), padding his lead. In front of the hometown crowd at Phoenix, Bryan finished second in the last race of the season and topped off his lead with another 160 counters to win the inaugural USAC National Championship with a 360 point margin. This also gave Bryan the distinction of being the first driver to be crowned champion by both the AAA and the USAC. Flaherty still took second with 1,500 points, while Freeland ended in third with 1,250.

Here Comes The Jud
September 2, 1957

The 1957 championship racing season opened its 11th year since the end of World War II with Sam Hanks finally winning the Indianapolis 500. His triumph came 17 years after his first appearance at the Speedway in 1940. With the victory Hanks joined an elite group of drivers who had not only won the 500, but had also been national champions.

While Hanks immediately announced his retirement from the championship trail in victory lane (only to end up winning a NASCAR stock car race less than a month later), his victory in the 500 signaled another movement in the design of racing cars.

Hanks' winning car, the No. 9 Belond Exhaust Special, had been entered in the 500 by its owner George Salih, who also served as the machine's lead mechanic. Salih advanced the development of pavement roadsters another step when he had the Offenhauser engine tilted almost horizontally in an Epperly chassis to make the car even lower than its predecessor, the Kurtis. Wrapped in a sleek skin, the car sported a tailfin, an early effort of using a wing on a racing car. As a result, Hanks led three quarters of the race to his record 135.601 mph win.

Despite the constant technological improvements in the pavement championship cars, the dirt track races remained dominant on the 1957 USAC Championship schedule. Thirteen races were scheduled for the season and only four of them would be tarmac affairs. After Indy came Johnny Thomson's win on the dirt of Langhorne. Next, Roger Ward was victorious on the Milwaukee pavement. Bryan, who had secured 700 points with his third place finish in the 500, was the next winner on the dirt track in Detroit.

The pit crews, owners and drivers then loaded themselves and their cars into airplanes, and for the first time left the United States to race against the Grand Prix drivers of Europe and South America in a long awaited grudge match. The event, which was 500 miles in length, was held on Italy's 2.6 mile Monza oval (a race track consisting of 38-degree turns as opposed to the nine degree turns of Indianapolis Motor Speedway), and was won in dominant fashion by the Cowboy. Bryan fascinated the Italian fans with his rugged American West demeanor, and laid down a world record speed of 160.060 mph for his victory. While the race added to the prestige of Bryan as a driver, and to American championship racing overall, it did not award any points toward the driver's title, as it was one of two extra "exhibition" events added to the 1957 USAC schedule. The other would be a 25-lapper in Pennsylvania at Williams Grove Speedway in late July.

Returning to the American dirt tracks on the Fourth of July, it was George Amick of Venice, Calif. winning at Atlanta to post the third victory of his championship career. Amick had never driven in the Indianapolis 500, but he was a seasoned 12-year veteran of the championship trail.

At the Williams Grove exhibition race, Jud Larson proved he was no flash in the pan championship contender with his dominant victory. After winning his first champ car race in October of 1956 at Sacramento, the rough-and-tumble, hard-living Larson had been retained to drive the No. 2 John Zink Special for the entire 1957 season.

But, at the Illinois State Fair on August 17, it was Roger Ward who throttled the field and led every lap of the 100-miler. He was followed across the line by Larson.

Going on to the third championship pavement race at Milwaukee the next week, another winner emerged when Jim Rathmann posted his very first championship victory. He had finished just 21 seconds behind Hanks in the 500 driving car owner Lindsey Hopkins other car, the No. 26 Chiropractic Special.

By the time the big car circus arrived in Southern Illinois for the Ted Horn Memorial, the national championship points fight was up for grabs as seven different drivers had won the seven points paying races run thus far in the 1957 season.

That Magic Mile

The clincher was that Hanks, with the 1,000 points he had earned at Indy, would not appear. Nor would Rathmann, who had acquired 1,300 points on the strength of his win at Milwaukee, his second place at Indianapolis, and his fifth-place finish in the 100-miler held in June at Milwaukee. Rathmann was a pavement specialist, and he chose to take his chances at the title with only one asphalt race remaining in the season on a brand new track at Trenton, New Jersey.

That left Bryan leading the dirt track contingent with 960 points going into Du Quoin. The Cowboy had earned his points by finishing third at Indy, winning at Detroit, and finishing seventh in Springfield. He had not finished well enough in the other four races to earn any points at all. In fact, after Indianapolis, he sat out the race at Langhorne.

Next came Amick with a solid 880 points to trail the Cowboy. Then Larson with 540, while Ward possessed 400. That still gave both drivers a shot at the championship with six 100-mile races (including Du Quoin), remaining.

The Hayes family added new bleacher stands on either side of the main grandstand in time for the 1957 fair, and hundreds of tickets were purchased for the many coal miners and their families by the area's many mining operations. As a result, attendance figures indicated that more than 17,000 spectators would attend the race. This also explained why promoter "Buck" Kidd could boast of the $17,500 purse available to the drivers, an increase of almost $3,000 in just one year.

The fireworks began as Jud Larson qualified for the race in the John Zink Special with a new record speed of 101.209 mph, besting the previous record speed of 100.223 mph set by Tony Bettenhausen in 1949. Roger Ward came second with a 99.945 in the Lesovsky Wolcott entry, while Johnny Thomson brought the D-A Lubricant Kuzma up to third on the grid at 99.668. Don Branson would leave the line in fourth with a solid 99.338 in the now seven-year-old Basement Bessie.

The rest of the 18 starters made the show under 98.928 mph. Bryan would start sixth, while Amick sat far back in the tenth slot.

A slight rain delayed the start of the race for half an hour. When the cars finally took the green flag, Ward pulled way over to the outside of the track, took a bite of the dirt and grabbed the lead away from Larson. He was followed by Thomson and Bryan, and it remained the same until the fourth lap.

That's when the Cowboy lost control of his mount and flipped the Dean Van Lines Special while trying to get by Thomson in the third turn. Bryan and the car were turned upright and towed into the pits as the field cruised under the yellow flag for the next six laps. Bryan showed the sold out crowd what a champion driver was made of and simply shrugged off the trauma, had his tires changed, and returned to battle.

At the restart it was again Ward maintaining the lead over Larson, Thomson and Amick. At lap 22, Bryan retired with an out-of-whack front suspension system. His car had sustained much more damage from the roll than the Dean Van Lines crew had originally assessed.

Ward's lead began to fade due to a broken shock absorber, while Larson sat back and waited, conserving his tires for the remainder of the contest. On the 54th lap, Larson went for the kill and took the lead. On lap 66, Amicks No. 78 lost its engine, and his season-long record of top-ten finishes came to an end.

At lap 75, Thomson moved past the ailing Ward and took second, while Elmer George, who had started 12th, moved into fourth place, followed by Bob Veith.

It was Larson's show for the last 25 laps. He loved to drive on dirt tracks, and by the end of the race led the field by half a lap for the second points paying victory of his championship career. Thomson maintained second and was trailed across the finish line by the still limping Ward.

That Magic Mile

Despite his last place finish at Du Quoin, Bryan ended the season with four top-ten finishes and a victory at Phoenix, to give him a total of 1,650 points. The Cowboy would again take the national title, making him only the fourth ever three-time American driving champion, joining Earl Cooper, Louis Meyer and Ted Horn in that select group. Pavement driver Jim Rathmann fell 180 points shy of Bryan for second in the standings, while Amick was third with an even 1,400 markers.

Jud Larson took it all in Southern Illinois in 1957, grabbing the pole position and the second big car victory of his colorful career. Here he receives a well deserved trophy from Tony Hulman, the owner of the Indianapolis Motor Speedway.
(The Weatherford/Foutch Collection)

That Magic Mile

Johnny Be Good
September 1, 1958

For the first time in several years, the national championship season began with another race prior to the Indianapolis 500. Len Sutton, a midget driver from Portland, Oregon, who had passed his driver's test at Indy in 1956, won the 100-mile event on March 30 at the new, one-mile, paved track at Trenton, New Jersey.

The 1958 season employed a similar format as the year before with a total of 15 champ car events. As in 1957, two of those races would not award points, and again they would be held in Monza, Italy, and at Williams Grove, Penn. Nine races on the USAC calender would be held on dirt tracks with the remaining six run on the paved venues. With the exclusion of the dirt race at Detroit and an added event at Trenton in September, the amount of pavement races increased by one.

When round two ended at the Indianapolis Motor Speedway on Memorial Day, Jimmy Bryan finally added the jewel to his racing crown with his much anticipated victory behind the wheel of Salih's Epperly Offenhauser. Hanks had driven the car to victory the year before. The name of the car had been changed from the Belond Exhaust Special to the Belond AP Special. Other than that, the only other noticable changes to the car were the enlarged cockpit (to suit Bryan's larger frame), and the addition of four slim pockets sewn into the cockpit upholstery to carry the trademark cigars that the Cowboy would chew on over the course of 500 miles.

The glory of Bryan's victory was tempered only by his announcement that he would not attempt to go for a fourth championship title, and that he would only appear at Monza as the defending champion of an event that was now billed as "The Race of Two Worlds." For the rest of the season he would remain a spectator.

At the next race in Milwaukee, it was another relatively unknown midget car pilot named Art Bisch who was the surprising winner. Bisch had taken over as the the driver of the old, and infamous No. 81 Central Excavating Special that Sutton had failed to put into the starting field at Indianapolis.

"Fast Eddie" Sachs, the pixie-like racer from Center Valley, Penn., won the next event at Langhorne for the second victory of his big car career.

At the end of June it was back across the Atlantic for another showdown against the world's Grand Prix drivers at Monza. Jim Rathmann won the three-legged event as the Americans gave the European racers a sound thrashing for the second year in a row.

Returning to the states, Jud Larson (who did not travel to Italy) celebrated the Fourth of July weekend by winning the Atlanta 100. He then successfully defended his title in the non-championship race at Williams Grove on July 20.

Next, on the 16th of August, Johnny Thomson, throttled the field at Springfield and set a new speed record of 98.137 mph that would stand at that track for the next 24 years.

Back on the pavement at Milwaukee for the track's second race of the season, Roger Ward won the 200-miler and claimed the first of his two big-car victories of the year.

When only 25 cars arrived at Du Quoin for the Labor Day weekend the USAC National Championship points scenario had become a hotly contested affair. For the second year in a row the Indianapolis 500 winner would not appear. Bryan remained true to his word and savored the glory of his victory in the 500 while he sat out the season. His absence from Du Quoin - like that of Hanks in 1957 - became a moot point in the championship title chase. The 1,000 points he earned with the Indy win may have given him the points lead for a while, but by Labor Day he had been relegated to third in the standings, and by season's end he would drop to sixth.

In the foreground, A.J. Foyt and the Dean Van Lines crew prepare for time trials. Foyt started third and finished eighth the first time he qualified on the Du Quoin oval. (The Weatherford/Foutch Collection)

Leading the standings with 1,320 clickers was George Amick, of Rhinelander, Wis. The Indianapolis Rookie of the Year had finished second in his first appearance in the 500, and the dirt track ace obviously found pavement racing to his liking. He turned in four more top-ten finishes on asphalt tracks before his arrival at the Du Quoin fairground's oval.

Tony Bettenhausen, who also had not won a race in 1958, was second in the standings with 1,030 markers, largely due to his fourth place finish at Indy and two second place showings at Trenton and Milwaukee.

Fourth was Johnny Boyd, the latest Bowes Seal Fast driver, who finished third in the 500. At Milwaukee he was fifth; but at Langhorne with 800 points to his credit, his race car caught fire and he was critically burned and hospitalized for the remainder of the season.

Grouped almost together were the season's only other winners besides Bryan and Bisch. In fifth was Larson - now pushing the pedal of the Bowes Seal Fast car - with 630 points, followed by Thomson with an even 600. Sachs was in seventh with 590 and then came Ward with

Polesitter, Johnny Thomson and second place starter, Don Branson, were the only drivers to qualify at over 100 mph. (The Weatherford/Foutch Collection)

Running in third place during most of the race, Don Branson (10), leads Roger Ward (8) and Jud Larson (9) into the first turn. (The Weatherford/Foutch Collection)

460. With six races left in the season these four talented hot shoes were still very much in contention for the drivers' championship.

Ninth in the standings was a young driver named Anthony Joseph Foyt Jr., who would carry 390 points into Du Quoin. Hailing from Houston, Texas, the 23-year-old was known simply as "A.J." and was competing in his first full season on the championship trail, but he was turning heads. Starting his USAC career in 1956, driving his own midget car in three races at the one-quarter mile 16th Street Speedway in Indianapolis, he moved up to sprint and championship cars in 1957. That year he collected four top-ten finishes out of five sprint car starts. In the big champ cars he drove the Hoover Motor Express in five of the season's 13 races and garnered three Top 10 results. He failed to qualify at Du Quoin that year.

But Foyt caught the eye of Al Dean, the owner of the Dean Van Lines Special. The car had been sitting with an empty cockpit due to Bryan's prior commitment to Salih's Indy effort. Dean invited Foyt to take his Indianapolis rookie test in his car and the young Texan passed with flying colors. He started the 500 in 12th and finished in 16th place after spinning out on lap 148. Foyt's respectable rookie finish was clouded only by the death of his friend and fellow driver, Pat O'Connor, who died in a horrible 19-car accident at the start of the race.

Dean must have appreciated Foyt's aggressive driving style because he continued to retain A.J. after a disapointing 21st place finish in the next race at Milwaukee. However, Foyt showed remarkable improvement by the time one of Dean's moving vans pulled into the infield at Du Quoin with the No. 29 car on board. Foyt had placed second at Langhorne, 11th at both Atlanta and Springfield, and the week before at Milwaukee he had ended the race in seventh.

The Hayes' Du Quoin fair featured a unique triple bill for the first time in 1958. The auto racing weekend started off with Fred Lorenzen of Elmhurst, Illinois, winning the 100-mile stock car race. Roger Ward was the victor of the 100-mile midget race on Sunday.

Johnny Thomson collects his winning hardware from Tony Hulman as race promoter, Buck Kidd (in suit and tie) and USAC President, Tom Binford (with binoculars), look on.
(The Weatherford/Foutch Collection)

The combination of 200 racing miles already run on the Du Quoin oval insured that the track's surface would be tough on the big car's tires. Johnny Thomson grabbed the pole position with a speed of 100.643 mph in the D-A Lubricant Special, while Don Branson would start on the outside as the only other driver to edge past the 100-mph mark.

Starting third was Du Quoin rookie, Foyt, with his speed of 99.861. Then came Ward, Freeland, Larson, Earl Motter, Len Sutton, points leader Amick, and Bettenhausen, who rounded out the top-ten.

Sachs, the soon to become Midwest Sprint Car Champion, qualified in 13th, but almost lost his starting position when the rear end of his car went to pieces at the end of his two-lap time trial. But, Elmer George generously turned over the wheel of the No. 21 HOW Special to Sachs so that he could make the show, and remain in the points chase.

Thomson took off with a flawless start at the green and opened up a huge lead. Branson, driving the Hoover Motor Express, tried in vain to hold off Foyt.

By the end of lap two, Foyt was around Branson's orange car while Bettenhausen, piloting Larson's old Zink ride, was on the charge from tenth place.

With ten laps down it was still Thomson in command, followed by Foyt, Branson, Ward, Larson and Bettenhausen, who was already up to sixth.

After 20 laps the top three in the running order were the same. Larson was probably having misgivings about giving up the Zink car to Bettenhausen, as the Tinley Park Express had by now cruised into fourth.

Lap 27 had the fans in the packed grandstands on their feet as they saw Bettenhausen come around the fourth turn in second snipping at the heels of Thomson's No. 7 after getting by Branson and Foyt.

The front runners stayed in position for the next eight laps until the points leader, Amick, spun out in the third turn and backed his No. 3 Hopkins into the infield guardrail to block the racing line. The resulting yellow caution flag bunched up the field for the next 12 laps while Amick's car was pried free from the fence and removed from the track.

When Vandewater flew the green banner again, Thomson held his lead until the 56th time around. Then he encountered the slowing car of Sachs, who had lost the transmission in the HOW. Thomson moved high into the loose dirt and slowed as his Firestone tires lost grip in the marbles. Bettenhausen, who had hounded the Flying Scot since the restart, saw his only chance to get by the leader, and took it.

For the next 40 laps it was Bettenhausen, Thomson and Branson. Ward had moved into fourth after the restart and remained there since. Foyt, who had shown promise early on, had slowly faded and was now motoring along in eighth.

Thomson stayed glued to Bettenhausen's tail. The three-time Du Quoin winner couldn't pull away during the closing quarter of the race, and Thomson, who seemed to gain in the turns, would only loose ground on the straightaways. In an almost instant replay of the 47th lap, Thomson got his break. Bettenhausen went high after hitting a rut in the north turn. Thomson, down near the rail, sailed past and held tight for the last three laps to win the race and become the first two-time winner of the year.

Thomson had set another race speed record, was awarded $5,250 out of the $20,360 purse, and collected 200 points to move into a tie with the still hospitalized Boyd. At the end of the season, Thomson would wind up third in the standings. Bettenhausen took home $3,686 and moved within 170 points of Amick's points lead. Eventually, Bettenhausen would finish in the top-five positions of the last five races of the season, and beat out Amick by 190 points to clinch the driver's title. For the first time in the history of the national championship, a driver would take the crown without winning a single race over the course of an entire season.

Triple W
September 7, 1959

The Indy car season began with three races scheduled before the Indianapolis 500. A points paying 100-miler and a non-championship 50-mile contest were held on April 4, at the new two-and-a-half mile track at Daytona Beach, Florida. NASCAR's inuagural Daytona 500 stock car race had been won by Lee Petty there in February. In the champ car events, Jim Rathmann, the pavement specialist, won both races in the Simoniz Special with record speeds. In the 100-mile race, he posted a previously unheard of race speed of 170.261 mph. The Daytona Speedway quickly became known as the fastest racetrack on earth. Sorrowfully, the day was tainted by the death of George Amick, who died during the first race. The personable Amick had reached the point in his career where the versatility of his talent as a winning driver on both asphalt and dirt tracks was without question.

The big car circus then moved up the East Coast to Trenton for the third of seven pavement races scheduled for the 1959 season. Tony Bettenhausen was declared the winner of the event when it was stopped after 87 miles because of rain. By taking the checkered flag at Trenton, Bettenhausen logged the 20th big car victory of his 22-year racing career. He had won his first race in 1938 driving in a midget event at the Chicago Armory. He had twice been a National Champion, despite never achieving his lifetime goal of winning the Indianapolis 500.

Roger Ward won the Indy 500 after running what many considered one of the most perfect 500's to date. Three cars were on the lead lap at the end of the race. That had happened only once before in the 48-year history of the Memorial Day event. Ward completed the race with only three pit stops that averaged just 24 seconds each.

In fact, 1959 seemed to be adding up as Ward's year all the way around. He had finished second to Rathmann in the 100-mile race at Daytona. He was second again at Trenton. With the win at Indianapolis he was cushioned by his 200-point lead over Rathmann's 1,120. It didn't make much difference to the title fight when he was forced out of the next race at Milwaukee by a burned piston. The winner that day was Johnny Thomson.

Ward was driving for the Leader Card Duo team, which was owned by Bob Wilke. Mechanic A.J. Watson was responsible for the preparation of Ward's pavement and dirt cars, and was considered to be the top man in his profession. He had wrenched the cars that had won three of the last five Indy 500's. The three W's: Ward, Watson and Wilke, were the trio to beat in 1959.

Ward sat out the next race at Langhorne where Thomson crashed during practice. There was no change to the championship picture as Van Johnson came out of nowhere to collect his first big car win.

Back on dirt at Springfield in August, Jud Larson suffered a heart attack during qualifications for the race. It would sideline the the 37-year-old racing veteran for five years. Ward qualified in sixth for the Illinois state capital's annual event, but on the fourth lap of the race he dropped out with another burned piston in his Offenhauser motor. Again, it made no difference to his title hopes because Len Sutton emerged as the victor. Ward was still well in front of the point's chase.

A week later in the Milwaukee 200, Ward showed his championship style and the strength of the Leader Card Duo team when he charged from a 19th place starting position and won the race. The win only padded his domination of the point's standings with 400 extra markers.

Long time Du Quoin promoter, Buck Kidd, had died of a heart attack early in 1959 and his duties of organizing the fair's annual racing card were undertaken by William Hayes' grandson, Bill Hayes. The younger Hayes knew right away that his races would be successful. For the first time since 1955, when Bob Sweikert competed in the Ted Horn Memorial, the champ car race would feature the Indy 500 winner. Ward changed the pattern set by Hanks and Bryan and announced early on that he would indeed campaign the entire season. He headed the list of 27 entrants at Du Quoin.

That Magic Mile

Top qualifier, Don Branson (9) leads the field into turn one after the start of the 1959 Ted Horn Memorial. (The Weatherford/Foutch Collection)

The weekend started off with Fred Lorenzen winning the stock car race for the second year in a row, while Tony Bettenhausen took first the next day in the 100-mile midget race.

On Labor Day, well over 20,000 fans flooded the fairground to attend the big car clash between the knights of the round track. Don Branson went out and posted the day's only speed run over 100 mph with his clocking of 35.63. Ward couldn't do any better than a 99.037 mph run, but his speed was good enough for the outside of the first row.

Third on the grid was Thomson, looking for back-to-back wins, and in fourth was the Du Quoin newcomer and Indianapolis 500 Rookie of the Year, Bobby Grim. Fifth was the veteran, Big Don Freeland, the latest driver to sign with the Bowes Seal Fast's revolving door team. Sixth

That Magic Mile

fastest was Jack Turner, the 1954-55 National Midget Champion, followed by Len Sutton, Bob Veith, Jim McWithey, Eddie Sachs, and Tony Bettenhausen, who had again taken over driving duties in the Zink car for Larson.

Surprisingly, A.J. Foyt didn't make the cut in the Dean Van Lines car. He qualified last, but was displaced by his fellow Texan, Lloyd Ruby, who would start 18th driving the Texas Racing Club Offenhauser.

When Vandewater dropped the green, Ward dispelled any notion that his failure to take the pole was a sign of weakness. He launched the Leader Card Duo No. 5 right into the first turn, and left Branson with a face full of Du Quoin's calcium enriched dust. It was left up to Branson in the yellow and red No. 9 Estes to hold off the other 16 cars as Ward worked up a good advantage before the end of the first lap.

Round and round they went, lap after lap. By lap 34, Ward began to pass slower cars running at the back of the field. Meanwhile, Branson had his hands full as Grim hounded him with the No. 16 Hopkins. By lap 47, Bettenhausen had moved into fourth with the Zink, disposed of Grim, and prepared to take his best shot at Branson for second.

For the second year in a row Sachs dropped out of the race. This time it was engine failure on the 45th lap that sidelined him. On lap 53, the three-time National Midget Champion, Shorty Templeman, hit the guardrail but escaped injury.

Pit stops were not even a factor during the race, and the only stop for service was made by the defending Du Quoin champion, Thomson, who developed tire trouble at lap 67 and dropped out.

After leading every lap of the race, Ward was waved by the checkered flag for the third time that year. He would take home $5,450 of the purse and receive another 200 points for working on a holiday. He now had 1,920 points toward winning the driver's trophy at the end of the year. His nearest challenger, Rathmann, had suffered a concussion after flipping a sports car the day before in a race at the new road course

Roger Ward led every single lap of the 1959 race. (Courtesy of the Indianapolis Motor Speedway).

track located outside of Chicago at Meadowdale. It was not known if he would race again that year.

Ward went on to win one more race that season and finished third in two others to end the season as the National Champion with 2,400 points. Bettenhausen won the 21st race of his career later that year in Phoenix and finished second to Ward with 1,430. This put Bettenhausen ahead of Bryan 10,595.5 to 9,681.4 as the all-time career point's leader. Thomson ended right behind in the season standings with 1,400 despite not racing in the last four events that year. Rathmann, who competed in only four races during the entire season, amassed 1,154.8 points to finish fifth. A.J. Foyt was sixth with 910.2 markers, due to his six top-ten finishes.

The Changing of the Guard
September 5, 1960

1960 appeared once again to be a year for Roger Ward. Still the number one driver for the Leader Card team, Ward started off the season with a victory at Trenton and then placed second behind Jim Rathmann in an extremly competitive Indy 500. At Milwaukee he won again and had a 200 point lead over Rathmann by the time the big cars arrived at Langhorne in mid June. Neither Ward nor Rathmann would drive at the Pennsylvania track. Rathmann only drove pavement races and Ward thought Langhorne to be a bit on the dangerous side. Full of potholes, the one-mile dirt track was so rough that one of its corners was nicknamed "Puke Hollow" by the drivers. Over the years it had taken the lives of several championship contenders.

Jimmy Bryan decided that he would come out of semi-retirement for the Langhorne race and was offered the empty cockpit of Ward's No. 1 car for the event. It was a mistake. Bryan, who feared nothing, crashed to his death on the very first lap, and the 1960 Indianapolis Rookie of the Year, Jim Hurtubise, collected a sad victory for his first big car win.

At Springfield in August, Ward failed to make the field by just 12/100's of a second and his good fortune began to change. He still retained the points lead after second year champ car pilot Jim Packard won the Illinois State Fair race. But a week later at Milwaukee, Ward dropped out halfway through the 200-miler with mechanical problems and scored no points. Len Sutton won the race, while A.J. Foyt came in second. By now Foyt trailed Rathmann's 1,000 points for second in the standings with 600, as Ward continued in the lead with 1,200.

Foyt had switched from the Dean Van Lines team for the 1960 season and was now the latest driver for the Bowes Seal Fast squad. The team was co-owned by Bob Bowes, an Indianapolis-based manufacturer of automotive chemicals, and chief mechanic George Bignotti, who would tune many of Foyt's race cars for years to come.

Again, more than 20,000 fans paid their admission and this time 33 cars showed up at Du Quoin for the 14th running of the Ted Horn Memorial. Fair manager and promoter Bill Hayes was so enthused that he began to entertain the idea of holding two big car races on the same weekend, as was the case in 1951. He could not explain why, but it was obvious to Hayes that the crowd strongly preferred the roaring champ cars over the stock cars, midgets or even motorcycles that over the years had raced at Du Quoin.

Driving the Bob Estes No. 7, Don Branson bettered Jud Larson's 101.209 mph run set in 1957 with a blistering 104.469 speed in qualifications. He easily held the pole position through the remainder of time trials. Lloyd Ruby, the latest driver in the J.C. Agajanian stable, couldn't even nudge Branson's clocking with his two-lap average of 102.799, but it was good enough for second in the lineup. In third came the hot newcomer Hurtubise with a 101.868, while Foyt duplicated the run with the exact same clocking. Fifth was another Texan named Al "Cotton" Farmer, a rookie who had finished fourth at Langhorne.

Sixth on the grid was Packard. The winner of the Springfield race, he was known as a real crowd pleaser because of his aggressive style of driving high in the turns, while other drivers usually took the conventional lower groove on the tracks. Finishing no worse that sixth in the four races he had run in 1960, Packard, a resident of Speedway, Indiana, was known to slice his way from the back of the pack with reckless abandon. He was fourth in the points standings with 540, just 60 behind Foyt.

Starting seventh was the old master of Du Quoin, Tony Bettenhausen. That year he was driving the No. 2 Dowgard entry. Eighth was Gene Force in the Tiz-So, followed by Bobby Grim, while Johnny Thomson, having a rather dismal season, was tenth in the Hoover Motor Express. Eleventh was a disapointed Ward, whose run of bad luck seemed to be getting worse. In the 12th spot was Du Quoin rookie Parnelli Jones. His best showing thus far on the championship trail was a sixth place finish at Langhorne. Behind Jones was Shorty Templeman, the three-time midget champion still trying to make his mark in the big cars, while Sachs and another Du Quoin rookie named Chuck Hulse rounded out the top 15 starting positions. All had bettered the 100-mph mark.

Tony Bettenhausen finished second in his final appearance at Du Quoin in 1960. (The Phil Harms Collection)

In 16th was the 1952 Du Quoin winner, Chuck Stevenson, who had ended the retirement brought on by the death of Clay Smith in 1954. His come-back was made with a surprising appearance in the Indy 500 as Ward's Leader Card teammate. In 17th was Elmer George, returning to Southern Illinois after finishing third at Springfield. Starting last was Roger McCluskey, an Arizona stock car racer in his first year of USAC competition. He had placed fifth at Langhorne and turned in a 99.065 mph run in his qualification bid.

As expected, at the start it was Branson in control of the field. Maintaining his lead, the part-time cab driver lead the first 50 miles of the race with considerable ease, and was ahead by as much as half a lap. But Packard was roaring up from sixth picking off one driver after another.

Meanwhile Jones had dropped out on the 19th lap. On lap 34 both Stevenson and Ward were out of the action. Again, Ward was the victim of mechanical woes. The 1959 champion's luck was wearing thin. Ten laps later McCluskey and George found themselves in the pits and out of the race.

On lap 57 Packard had closed on Branson and picked him off in the south turns. Packard thrilled the crowd after going full throttle into turn one and then taking the high side all the way through turn two, giving Branson a classic "rim ride." Branson was suffering from a misfiring Offenhauser and found himself being passed by Foyt and Hurtubise by the 70th lap.

Packard played the dangerous tire game but continued to stretch his lead over second place Foyt. In third was Hurtubise, who cruised into the pits on lap 74 and did not appear on the track again.

After three-quarters of the way the running order of the top five was Packard, Foyt, Branson, Bettenhausen and Farmer. On lap 76, Packard realized that his right rear tire was literally coming apart at the seams. He pitted for fresh rubber and gave up the lead to Foyt. On lap 77 Gene Force spun his Tiz-So Special into the north turn guardrail and the car

After winning the first of an all-time record 67 National Championship Indy car events, a happy A.J. Foyt talks to the Du Quoin crowd. (Photo by C.V. Haschel. Courtesy of A.J. Foyt)

That Magic Mile

burst into flames. The yellow waved for the next ten laps. Force received severe burns to his hands

Still under the caution, Packard rejoined the field. When the green flew to signal the restart he began a determined charge back toward the front. On one lap he came out of the fourth turn so hard he banged the rail - sending fans running for their lives. Luckily, he kept the car under control and zoomed down the straightaway in pursuit of Foyt. But A.J. wouldn't be denied. Confident that he would be the winner, he threw caution to the wind and put his foot to the floor. He won his first ever championship race on the track that he would get to know well over the next 14 years.

Foyt finished a full lap ahead of second place Bettenhausen, who was followed by Farmer, Sachs, and Packard. For the victory, Foyt received $5,165 of the $20,195 purse. But of much more importance was that he gained another 200 points and closed to within 400 of Ward for the driver's title.

Ward's season went down the drain after Du Quoin. He could muster only two more points-paying finishes over the rest of the season with a second at Trenton and a tenth at Phoenix. Foyt, however, took the points lead with just two races remaining on the USAC schedule with his win at Sacramento and settled the issue once and for all with another victory at the season ending race in Phoenix.

Within the month, the hard charging Packard's career came to a tragic end when he was killed in a midget race at Fairfield, Illinois. The Flying Scot, Johnny Thomson, also was killed less than a month later while racing at Allentown, Penn.

On A Roll
September 4, 1961

1961 looked like the year for Eddie Sachs when he won the opening event of the champ car season at Trenton for the third year in a row. The New Jersey fairground track was firmly stamped as the likable Sachs' private domain, as he had become the track's only three-time winner in its brief national championship history. Sachs, still driving for Al Dean, would prove to be a major contender in the chase for the year's driving title. He proved this when he won the assault on the coveted pole-position of the year's Indianapolis 500, an event that was celebrating its Golden Jubilee.

Tony Bettenhausen, who was planning an attempt to qualify for his 15th consecutive Indianapolis 500 was killed on May 12th, the day before time trials were scheduled to begin. The extremely popular driver died while testing the car that would be driven by his old friend, Paul Russo. Bettenhausen would be missed. In his long career as a driver, he had never won the 500, but twice he had been crowned as the national driving champion and at the time of his death, was the all-time national championship points leader with a total of 11,535.5 career markers. Always favored by the fans in Southern Illinois, he was Du Quoin's only three-time winner.

That year's 500 was both the fastest ever run, and the race's closest-ever finish, but it was also the fiercest-faught in the Speedway's 50-year history of automotive combat. Sachs, Foyt, Ward, Jim Hurtubise, Jim Rathmann, Troy Ruttman and rookie Parnelli Jones each led a portion of the race. However, it was the current national champion, Foyt, who would emerge with his likeness etched on the Borg-Warner trophy for the first time in his long and illustrious career.

Indy, run for the last time on its brick surface (it was due to be paved with asphalt in October) also featured for the first time, the appearance of a racing car with its motor mounted in the rear of the vehicle, behind the driver.

Eddie Sachs was second in the 1961 points chase when the Indy car circus arrived in Du Quoin. (The Phil Harms Collection)

The car was a version of the Cooper-Climax grand prix car that had carried Jack Brabham to back-to-back World Driving Championships in 1959 and 1960. Brabham, an Australian, had entered the 500 for the prestige of a possible victory and was attracted by the $400,000 purse, the richest in motorsports. Brabham put the little formula-one car into the 13th starting position on the first day of qualifications for the 500. Then, in his quest for a third consecutive world driving title he flew to Europe immediately afterward to compete in the Grand Prix of Monte Carlo, scheduled for the following day.

Returning to Indianapolis for Memorial Day, Brabham finished the race in ninth, proving at once that the rear-engined formula-one cars could contend with the heavy front-engined Indy roadsters. Though not as powerful on the Indianapolis straightaways as the conventional Offenhauser-powered car, the Climax-engined Cooper could make up for its lack of horsepower and scoot through the Speedway's long turns considerably faster than the cigar-shaped brutes all champ car drivers were accustomed to. The introduction of the rear-engine car and its solid finish at the Indianapolis 500 that year would eventually be considered as the single most important catalyst for change in American automobile racing history. By 1971, all Indy-car races would be run by rear-engined cars on paved venues. Not good news for the big car fans, promoters, and dirt track owners like the Hayes family, who placed stock in the popularity of their annual championship event. It was an especially dimmer experience for some car owners, who during the next decade would have to field three separate types of racing cars in order to compete for the championship crown. Even more difficult would be the task of finding drivers who could deal with the three-fold task of piloting the distinctly different machines.

Foyt, who during the next few years would lead the resistance against the rear-engined revolution, was 200 points behind Sachs when the champ cars arrived in Milwaukee for the 100-miler. But it was Ward, who had finished third in the 500 that won the race. Sachs did not start and Foyt wound up 22nd. But at Langhorne, where Ward steadfastly refused to even attempt a qualification run and at a track that even Foyt didn't care for, the young Texan proved he wasn't out of contention when he brought the Bowes Seal Fast Special home first and took over the points fight with a margin of 160 over Sachs.

Like others before him, Foyt was finally enjoying a season that many young drivers could only wish for. He had won Indy and continued to pad his points lead with a string of top-five finishes. He finished third and second respectively in the Milwaukee 200, and in the 100-mile Springfield race that was now labeled as the Tony Bettenhausen Memorial. By the time Labor Day rolled around, Foyt possessed a comfortable lead of 370 points over Sachs as they headed into the annual holiday weekend of racing at Du Quoin.

Monday began as a scorcher and by 11 a.m. the temperature was already 93 degrees. When track announcer, Ed "Twenty Grand" Steinbock, reviewed the starting lineup for the more than 20,000 sweltering fans who surrounded Du Quoin's oval, it was Jim Hurtubise who sat on the inside front row starting position for the 1961 race with his fast speed of 103.687 mph.

Driving the No. 56 Sterling Plumbing entry, Hurtubise was also enjoying a good season after winning his first race of the year at Springfield two weeks previously. Foyt would start second, while another future star named Parnelli Jones would take off third. Jones, the 1961 Indianapolis Co-Rookie of the Year, Foyt and Hurtubise were well-known to each other as they regularly competed in the USAC's Sprint Car division. With this in mind, the Du Quoin race promised to be a hotly contested affair.

Rookie, Chuck Hulse, hailing from California would begin his race in fourth driving the Tassi Vitas entry, while the always tenacious Ward, in the Leader Card machine would leave the line in fifth.

Nothing could spoil Foyt's Labor Day parade and the Texan slipped by Hurtubise in the first turn even before the green flag stopped waving. He was bound and determined to win the race on the track that had propelled him into stardom a year ago. Jones maintained third, and Hulse stayed put in fourth for the next thirty laps.

Ward had dropped from fifth to eighth by the end of the first 10 laps, but was back up into sixth despite suffering from unknown mechanical woes.

On lap 34 Hurtubise took a much anticipated shot at Foyt's lead, but instead looped his mount in the north turn, almost taking out Bobby Marshman and the struggling Ward, who both continued as the incident brought out the caution flag for the next seven laps.

Hurtubise's spin also dashed Foyt's attempt to break the race speed record of 94.75 mph set by Johnny Thomson in 1958. Foyt had driven the first quarter of the race in just 15-minutes, but as a result of the yellow, Thomson's clocking of 1:03.19 would stand.

Hot shoe, Jim Hurtubise (56), qualified at over 103 mph for the 1961 race. Above he follows the pace car prior to the start. (Courtesy of the Terry Weatherford/Keith Foutch Collection)

When the green waved again, the 26-year old Foyt jumped on the gas. Jones remained right on his tail. Hulse, the rookie, was driving a fine race and remained in third.

The notorious Southern Illinois heat became a factor for the next 50 laps as the race settled into its pace. Ward pitted for the day on lap 40. Next out was Lloyd Ruby on lap 41, then Roger McClusky joined the also-rans on the very next lap. Elmer George was sidelined on lap 55 and Cotton Farmer was gone on the 62nd.

At the three-quarter mark Foyt still led, but just barely over Jones.

Shorty Templeman, who had started 16th was now up to third. Hulse had dropped back into sixth, but continued at a steady pace with the front runners. Marshman, who had begun the race in tenth, was now fourth, while Sachs ran fifth after a ninth-place start. He needed better than a fifth-place finish to keep within range of Foyt in the points battle.

That Magic Mile

Hurtubise gets it sideways in the Sterling Plumbing Special as he passes Cotton Farmer.
(The Weatherford/Foutch Collection)

Hurtubise ended his own race on lap 34 after a spin that stalled his engine. Bobby Marshman (44) and Roger Ward (2) avoid the out-of-control car.
(The Weatherford/Foutch Collection)

On the 86th lap Jones got by A.J. Some suspected that Foyt's rapid pace, combined with the intense track temperature may have taken its toll on the Bowes Seal Fast Special. But Foyt remained on the track while Jones shot into a quarter-mile lead and appeared to be the sure winner with just 10 laps remaining. Foyt would not give in and hounded the leader. Jones pushed the pedal of his Agajanian Willard car one last time before his Offenhauser engine could take no more, and with a plume of smoke trailing behind him took the slow left turn into the infield.

Foyt took the checkered at Du Quoin for the second time in a row. He now joined Sam Hanks and Jimmy Bryan as the only two-time winners in Southern Illinois.

Templeman rolled home in second while Sachs picked up a badly needed 140 points for third.

But, it would not be enough. Foyt still led Sachs by over 400 points. The next race at Syracuse less than a week later left the title fight in the same position as Sachs failed to qualify and Foyt surprisingly, finished last.

Foyt won the next round at the Indiana State Fairground's "Hoosier Hundred" after passing Jones on the 16th lap and further extended his points lead over Sachs considerably, but Sachs countered with a win at Trenton (his fourth on that track), while Foyt could only complete 66 of the 100-miles scheduled.

Foyt finished no-better than 12th in the final two races of the season at Sacramento and Phoenix. Sachs competed in only the last affair at the Arizona track but could only muster a sixth-place finish for just 80-points.

No matter. Foyt claimed his second national championship in fine fashion. As the team leader for the Bignotti Bowes operation, he had brought home everything in 1961. The win at Indy, the national championship crown and the team's eighth victory in just two seasons. There would be many more to come.

Once is not enough. A.J. Foyt receives his trophy after becoming the third two-time victor of the Ted Horn Memorial in 1961. (The Weatherford/Foutch Collection)

The Flying Texan
September 2, 1963

Roger Ward won both the Indianapolis 500 and the national championship for the second time driving for the Leader Card team in 1962. Since 1959, Ward and Foyt had owned the title between themselves and five races into the 1962 season it was obvious that the story would remain the same. Foyt took the season opener at Trenton and Ward emerged as the victor in the 500 after Parnelli Jones suffered a failed brake line while holding a commanding lead for more than half the distance. Jones, the 1961- 62 USAC sprint car champion had become the first man in the history of the Speedway to qualify at over 150 mph. Foyt spun out of the race on the 70th lap after losing a wheel in the southeast turn.

In the next two races at Milwaukee and Langhorne, Foyt was first again. Ward came back for another victory at Trenton and it looked like the combination of Ward, Wilke and Watson would reign supreme again. Foyt and Jones each won another race during the rest of the season. But it was Ward, who missed the final two races at Sacramento and Phoenix because of an injury sustained in a road racing accident, who had accumulated 2460 points at season's end to take the driver's title. Foyt produced 1950 clickers for second place at the end of the year despite switching over to the Lindsey Hopkins stable at mid-season.

There was no Indy car event at Du Quoin in 1962. Heavy rains moved into Southern Illinois just in time to spoil the planned Labor Day weekend of sprint, stock and big car racing.

The sprint car dash scheduled for Saturday was an instant wash out. Many of the drivers entered were also slated to compete in the big car feature on Monday so they made themselves comfortable at the St. Nicholas Hotel in downtown Du Quoin and played cards as they waited out the weather. Some of them, including Foyt and Ward were pulling both double and triple duty and were due to race Sunday in USAC's national championship stock car race and then on Monday in the big cars. The stock car race got off the ground successfully after the fairground's track crew made a valiant attempt to work the dirt dry on the oval track. The 100-mile mudslinger was won by Paul Goldsmith in a Pontiac. He went on to become the national stock car champion for the second year in a row after winning eight of USAC's 20 scheduled fender-benders.

On Monday the skies opend up again and the big cars were placed under wraps or in the trailers that were being used by more and more competitors to haul their equipment from race to race. After discussions between the USAC and fair officials, it was agreed to attempt to run the race on Tuesday.

The next day, as the cars were being prepared for their qualification runs, Mother Nature let loose with a deluge and that was it. The fans would have their money reimbursed.

The Ward-Foyt championship scenario was much the same mid-way through the 1963 season. By the time the champ car circus left Springfield for the year's seventh race at Milwaukee, Foyt had three victories compared to Ward's two. "The Flying Texan," as Foyt was now known, had appeared in victory lane twice at Trenton and once at Langhorne while Ward, "The Silver Fox" had stood highest on the podiums at Milwaukee and at the Illinois State Fair. They were upstaged only by Jones, who proved that his strong run at Indianapolis the year before was no fluke when he repeated his performance with the No. 98 Agajanian Willard car. This time around, he bettered his previous 150-mph qualification run with a four lap average of 151.153 mph.

He also held off a much anticipated assault on the leading position of the race by the rear-engined contingent represented prominently by Colin Chapman's Lotus cars driven by the 1962 World Champion, Jimmy Clark, and regular Formula One competitor, Dan Gurney, of California. This time around, the rear-engined cars were powered by Ford motors, and at one time Clark's car led the race for more than 25 laps. After Jones had regained the lead his car began to leak oil onto the

Roger Ward set a new qualifying standard of 105.36 mph and broke Don Branson's 1960 record of 104.47 mph. Here the two drivers pace the field before the start. (The Weatherford/Foutch Collection)

track but he was never black-flagged, much to the dissapointment of Chapman, who believed that the Speedway officials were showing favoritism to one of their own. Jones went on to win the race.

Chapman and Clark returned from Europe in August to prove their point and set both pole and race speed records in the 200-miler run at Milwaukee. They vowed to return to Indianapolis until the little green race cars wound up in victory lane.

Next on tap was the race at Du Quoin. Ward went out and laid down a clocking of 34.17 for a new qualifying speed of 105.359 mph. That broke the record set by Don Branson in 1960 of 104.469. Branson, now

Parnelli Jones (98) laps Mickey Shaw's Chevrolet powered No.66 Lil-Beanie. Jones finished sixth while Shaw finished 15th in his only Du Quoin appearance. (The Weatherford/Foutch Collection)

Ward's teammate on the Leader Card team would start second for his 65th appearance in a USAC championship event. So far in the 1963 season he had won two sprint car features and two midget car races. Branson also finished third in the big cars at Springfield and had taken fifth in the 500. If ever a driver was due to win, it was Branson. Jim Hurtubise would easily make the show in third. Chuck Hulse, returning to Du Quoin after his solid rookie appearance in 1961 was in the fourth slot and Foyt, now driving under the Sheraton-Thompson banner, would begin his race in fifth.

Lining up for sixth was another Texan, Johnny Rutherford, of Fort Worth. He had passed his rookie test at Indianapolis and finished 29th in the 1963 race. Seventh was still another Texan, Jim McElreath of Arlington. In only his second year of national championship competition, this 35-year-old sensation had finished sixth in his first two Indianapolis 500's. Eighth would be DuQuoin veteran Bobby Marshman, followed by Jones and newcomer Bobby White, who rounded out the top 10.

As the field rolled down the front straight towards the green Hurtubise picked up speed and snuck past Branson at the start. He then took a grab for the lead from Ward in the first turn. Ward held firm and began to open up a huge lead over the next few laps. Only Foyt could keep pace and by lap 20 was beginning to catch up. Ward still held tight but on the 35th lap Foyt was right on his tail. The fans knew it wouldn't be long before their favorite driver would dice with Ward for the lead. And it wasn't. In just seven more laps Foyt was in the lead and beginning to stretch it out. At the halfway point Lloyd Ruby, who had started 13th, blew up his engine in a big way and brought out the yellow flag. But just briefly. As Ruby's car rolled to a stop on the outside of the south turns it was obvious that slowing the race was not going to be necessary and the green was flying before the end of the lap.

Foyt was hard on the gas and he lengthened his lead steadily to almost a full mile. Ward was no longer a threat. The only problem Foyt would encounter during the closing laps was a dwindling fuel supply. But the young Texan nursed it home and still broke Thomson's race

Three's a charm. A.J. Foyt again accepts his trophy from Tony Hulman. Foyt led the last 58 laps of the 1963 Ted Horn Memorial and set a new record race speed of 95.23 mph that broke Johnny Thomson's 1958 speed of 94.75 mph. (The Weatherford/Foutch Collection)

record with his third win in a row at Du Quoin. With the victory A. J. not only took home a healthy $5,587 for a half an hour's worth of work, but was now tied with Bettenhausen as a three-time winner of the Ted Horn Memorial.

Foyt still led in the points battle with an even 2200. Ward, who finished second followed with 1610, while Jones came in sixth and maintained third place in the points with 1410 on the strength of his 500 victory.

Chuck Hulse improved his Du Quoin record with a solid third and was followed across the finish line by Bobby Marshman and Branson.

Foyt took the championship title for the third time after the final race at Phoenix in 1963 and was quickly becoming known as the greatest racing driver ever to appear on the American scene.

That Magic Mile

Cleaning Clocks
September 7, 1964

Foyt began the 1964 season the same way he closed out 1963 as the points leader after the first of 13 races with a victory at Phoenix. Winning again in the following race at Trenton after starting from the pole, Foyt carried the momentum to Indianapolis but could only muster a fifth-place start in the 500-mile classic. Jimmy Clark returned in one of the 11 entered rear-engined cars and laid down a qualifying speed of 158.828 mph to secure the pole.

With the race less than two laps old tragedy struck. Rookie driver Dave MacDonald spun his rear-engined Sears-Allstate sponsored car coming onto the front stretch and hit the inside wall. The car, carrying a full tank of highly volatile blended gasoline exploded in front of Eddie Sachs, who rammed into MacDonald's blazing car and likewise went up in flames. Five more cars were also involved in the carnage and the race was halted. Sachs was dead. MacDonald died shortly thereafter, while another driver, Ronnie Duman, was burned so seriously his promising career was sidelined for several seasons. It was the Speedway's worst tragedy ever.

When the race resumed Bobby Marshman had the lead but he was losing oil and had to retire. Clark again took the helm. The Scotsman led the race until lap 47 when a chunk of rubber from a tire on his Lotus Ford shredded and mangled his rear suspension, ending his day. Parnelli Jones then had the lead, but a fire after a refueling stop on lap 55 sent him to the infield hospital. Foyt led for the next 145 laps to win for the second time. What most impressed the fans was that the 29-year old driver won the race driving what he called the "Old Antique" Sheraton-Thompson Special. A front-engined roadster. When the 11 rear-engined cars qualified for the 500, the experts had predicted that 1964 was the year that they would be victorious. They were wrong. Roger Ward came in second in the rear-engined Kaiser Aluminum car that was entered by the Leader Card team.

Don Branson raced in Southern Illinois from 1956 until 1966. (Courtesy of the Indianapolis Motor Speedway)

It was on to Milwaukee a week later and it was Foyt again in the winner's circle while a rear-engine car driven by Len Sutton came in second. Foyt made it five in a row at Langhorne and then six in the second race of the season at Trenton. He could not be stopped and to prove it the Texas racer brought the Sheraton Thompson Special home first again at Springfield after starting 16th, snapping his jinx on the only track where victory had eluded him.

Seven wins in seven races. It had never been done before. Not only was Foyt making history, he was also making points and money that year. With 2,300 points he led Roger Ward by more than 1000 markers and had pocketed a total of more than $187,694.00 to easily make him at that time the highest paid professional athlete in the world.

That Magic Mile

Cars are lined up and ready to qualify for the 1964 Ted Horn Memorial. (The Weatherford/Foutch Collection)

Mario Andretti made his first appearance on the Magic Mile in 1964 and qualified 11th in the Dean Van Lines machine. (The Jim Pursell Collection)

With six races remaining on the 1964 USAC Championship schedule Foyt changed cars for the next event at Milwaukee. He would finally try his hands on the wheel of a rear-engine car for the first time in competition. The Sheraton Thompson team prepared well and Foyt put the Lotus-Ford into third place on the starting grid, but when the race began the car was stuck in first gear and A.J. finished dead last after completing just one lap. Parnelli Jones won the race and Foyt returned to the cockpit of "The Old Antique" when the champ cars arrived at Du Quoin.

Again, the Hayes' fair would provide three days of USAC racing and continue to be the only track in the country to do so. Don Branson went out and broke Ward's qualification record and secured the pole.

A.J. would start second with Jones in third. Bobby Marshman would begin in fourth followed by Ward, Johnny Rutherford, and Jud Larson, who was making his return to racing that season. Eighth starter was Arnie Knepper of Belleville, Illinois, making the second appearance close to his home. Ninth would be Len Sutton with Jim McElreath in tenth. Starting 11th was rookie driver, Mario Andretti, competing in his first year on the championship trail as the driver of the Dean Van Lines entry. In 12th was Norm Hall, with Dee Jones starting next. Bobby Unser would start 14th. All three of these drivers were Du Quoin rookies. Next came Ralph Liguori, followed by stock car ace, Joe Leonard. Bud Tinglestad, who had finished 12th in his first race at Du Quoin a year ago was 17th. Lloyd Ruby rounded out the traditional field of 18.

At the start, Dee Jones' Windmill Truckers Special stalled and was pushed off the course, while Branson saw his pole advantage came to a quick end when he slowed briefly in the first turn of the race to let both Foyt and Marshman speed past.

Foyt, in the "Old Antique" and Marshman, driving the Hopkins Special, began to burn up the track. Lap after lap the two drivers ran away from the field with Branson struggling to keep pace. Ward and Jones were already a distant fourth and fifth as the race settled into its rhythm.

On lap 18 Lloyd Ruby turned for the pits and parked his machine for the day. The heat would again prove to be a factor in the race. Lap 31 saw Jones fall from contention as he retired.

Lap 40 saw Joe Leonard climb out of the appropriately named Konstant Hot Special to get relief from the already sidelined Dee Jones. Len Sutton pulled in two laps later as Ruby provided relief for the rookie driver. Andretti nursed the Dean Van Lines car into the pits on lap 45 to come up short the first time at Du Quoin. He did not seek help from another driver. His problems were mechanical, but he would be heard from again in Southern Illinois.

Foyt was still in the lead and looking for an unprecedented 25th championship victory. By now, both Foyt and Marshman had lapped

One more time! A.J. Foyt broke his own 100-mile race record by more than two-mph in 1964 for his fourth victory at Du Quoin. (Southern Illinoisan Photo)

the entire field. At the rate A.J. was traveling on the oval, along with a clean race, he was well on his way to breaking his own record, and about to become Du Quoin's first four-time winner.

The fans were in a frenzy of anticipation. Jones came in for the second time on lap 84, followed by Ward, who would also surrender his car to the heat as he pulled off the track on the very next lap.

Foyt burned up the oval over the next 15 laps and with his win blazed to a new track record of 97.80 mph, bettering his 1963 speed of 95.23. He was now Du Quoin's only four-time victor and with the win was ahead enough in the points chase to become the first ever four-time national driving champion. No one had a chance to catch him.

Finishing behind A.J. was Marshman (the only driver on the same lap), and Branson. Newcomer Bobby Unser cruised to fourth place, three laps down, and Jim McElreath came in fifth.

Branson (5) leads the starting field past the packed north bleachers after setting a new qualifying record speed over 106 mph. Foyt (1) on the outside would lead all 100 laps of the race.

Bobby Unser (8) qualified 14th for his first race at Du Quoin in 1964 and finished an impressive fourth. Jud Larson (97) started seventh and finished sixth in his comeback appearance. (The Weatherford/Foutch Collection)

Methuselah
September 6, 1965

The fate of national championship dirt car racing was sealed when Jimmy Clark finally captured the Indianapolis 500 crown in 1965 behind the wheel of the rear-engined Lotus Ford. The trend toward using rear-engined cars had been in progress for the last few years. Twenty-seven of the 33 qualifying cars in the 1965 500 carried their motors behind the driver. The movement to the smaller and lighter cars was also evident when the treacherous Langhorne track was repaved with asphalt during the off-season. The popularity of the big dirt cars was in decline. Attendance was going down at the dirt tracks and so were the purses. However, car owners still required different types of cars to compete for the national title and as long as the USAC's national championship calendar included dirt races, they were forced to maintain a stable that included front and rear engined machines.

This was good news for the Du Quoin State Fair. The Hayes' fairground had considered paving the dirt oval, but the point was moot as horse racing was still the predominant show at the fair. The Du Quoin fairground had held horse races since it opened and had been the site of Grand Circuit Harness racing since 1958. All during the week of the annual fair, horse races were held on an almost daily basis and would culminate with the running of the rich Hambletonian event, one of the most prestigious harness races in the world.

Once again the last three days of the fair were reserved for auto racing and twin 50-mile midget races were planned for Saturday. Sunday would again see the running of a 100-mile national championship stock car race and as tradition held, the big cars would take to the track on Monday.

As the racers arrived in Du Quoin, it was obvious that the chase for the national championship was still a wideopen affair. Nine drivers had won the 12 races already held of the 17 scheduled for the 1965 season. The year's Indianapolis 500 Rookie of the Year, Mario Andretti, led the points battle with 2,490 markers with Jim McElreath still very much in contention with 1,545. National Championship rookie, Gordon Johncock, of Hastings, Michigan was third in the standings with 1,510. Don Branson followed in fourth with 1,275 while A.J. Foyt stood fifth with 1,200. Jimmy Clark was frozen still with an even 1,000 points due to his victory at the 500 and his return to the Formula One circuit after the Memorial Day win. Parnelli Jones also stalled at 1000, followed by Joe Leonard (855), Lloyd Ruby (820) and Johnny Rutherford, who was tenth with 733.

With the exception of Ruby, all of these drivers had won at least one race thus far in 1965. Foyt and McElreath had emerged victorious twice. Andretti led in the points because of his ability to finish in the top six in 10 of the 12 races held. He had missed only one race in 1965 and finished 16th in the last race at Milwaukee.

Hungry for an unprecedented fifth consecutive win at Du Quoin, Foyt - who's season was not going as well as the year before - went out and put the old Sheraton Thompson Special on the pole and proved as usual he would take on all comers in Southern Illinois. Second would start Branson. Now a 45-year-old grandfather, Branson was the oldest driver in the field. Third was Jim Hurtubise. He had finished in the top 10 only three times thus far in 1965. Rutherford would begin fourth, Bobby Unser fifth, sixth was Jud Larson, seventh was Andretti, eighth would be Du Quoin rookie, Carl Williams. In ninth was Arnie Knepper, again making the short trip from Belleville, while another fresh face at Du Quoin, Gary Congden, rounded out the top 10.

Of note was the bid of rookie driver, George Morris, to put a rear-engined car into the field for the first time at Du Quoin. In a valiant effort, Morris qualified the Chevrolet powered Light Duty Racers Special dead last with a speed of 83.721 mph - far off the pace of Foyt's pole run of 103.211.

At the wave of the green Foyt maintained his lead for the first few laps. But a determined Branson passed him on the backstretch on the third trip around the oval. Branson held on tight as Foyt dogged him for

Foyt (1) and Branson (4) again held down the front row in 1965. (The Weatherford/Foutch Collection)

the next 30 laps, but the Texan was forced to enter the pits for fresh right rear rubber on lap 34.

Meanwhile, Morris, in the rear-engined car, had dropped out without completing a single lap. Attrition became a factor in the race and Unser was the next to drop out on the eighth lap, followed by Bud Tinglestad on lap 11. Andretti fell short on lap 14, while another Du Quoin rookie, George Snider, fell by the wayside on lap 16. Snider, of Bakersfield, Calif., had started in 12th driving the Agajanian-owned Hurst Floor Shifter Special. Knepper retired next on lap 22.

Branson was driving a beautiful race. Hot on his tail was McElreath followed by Foyt, who had fallen a full lap behind due to his pit stop, but was again on the charge.

Hurtubise had to be relieved by Unser on lap 40 because of heat exhaustion. On lap 60, Foyt again entered the pits for a new tire. On lap 78 the most thrilling piece of driving seen in a long time at Du Quoin was turned in by McElreath, who spun his Zink Trackburner Special in the north turns several times but gathered it up and maintained his second-place position.

On lap 85, the pace was slowed when two cars stopped on the track and the yellow flag flew for the next nine laps while the cars were removed from harm's way. The caution period destroyed any hope that Branson would set a new race record.

When the green flag appeared on lap 94 Branson kept his lead and six laps later rolled to his first national championship victory in his home state. He had come very close before. In the past, Branson had been second once at both Du Quoin and Springfield and twice third in Southern Illinois. Three times he had finished third at Springfield. Despite turning in the slowest race speed (88.792 mph) at Du Quoin since 1953, the "Dirt Track God" was jubilant with the win. He had ended Foyt's four-time domination of the event.

Don Branson finally won the Ted Horn Memorial after qualifying for the ninth straight time in 1965. Posing with his grandson for photographers, he is about to receive his trophy from Bill Hayes, the grandson of William R. Hayes. Notice the photo of Ted Horn to the right of Branson. (The Weatherford/Foutch Collection)

McElreath finished second on the same lap as Branson. A lap down in third was Foyt, who had made an amazing charge back up to the front. Fourth was veteran Jud Larson, while Johnny Rutherford placed fifth.

In 15th was Andretti, who went on to capture the championship title in 1965 despite only winning one race that year.

That Magic Mile

This Bud's For You
September 5, 1966

The United States Auto Club began its second decade as the sanctioning body of national championship racing in 1966 with a 15-race schedule. Jim McElreath won the season opener at Phoenix. Roger Ward took the checkered flag in the rain-shortened Trenton race a month later and would enjoy a brief 60 point lead over McElreath as the drivers headed to Indianapolis for the month of May.

When qualifying was over at the Indianapolis Motor Speedway, Mario Andretti had taken the Dean Van Lines Special to the pole position with a new record speed of 165.899 mph while Jimmy Clark held the second spot for the 500 mile classic. But, again it was another foreign driver who won the race. Englishman, Graham Hill, the 1962 World Driving Champion took the lead on the 191st lap of the crash-plagued 200-lap event and cruised the American Red Ball Special into victory circle. It would be the last time a foreign driver would win the 500 until 1989.

But Andretti still carried the numeral one on the nose of his race cars and the reason why was evident when the little Italian driver took down the pole spots in the next three races. Not only did Andretti start first at Milwaukee, Langhorne and at Atlanta, he also won the events and moved to within 220 points of McElreath, who was again leading the charge toward the championship. Andretti then went on to win the next race at Indianapolis Raceway Park to make it four in a row. Two weeks later at Langhorne's second race of the year he set a record qualifying lap and then crashed his Clint Brawner-Jim McGee prepared car on the second trip around the paved oval. Handing over the pole position to Don Branson in the Leader Card Racers Special, Andretti hopped into the cockpit of the Jim Robbins entry and put the car into the race despite never having driven it before. Starting 20th, Andretti could only manage to finish 33 of the scheduled 150 laps. Roger McCluskey took first in the race to prove that persistence pays off. The Tucson, Arizona resident had been competing on the championship trail since 1961 and finally scored his first victory.

In the points battle, Gordon Johncock moved into first on the strength of six top 10 finishes halfway through the season as the championship teams made ready for the Springfield race.

The race at the Illinois capitol started on a sad note when two photographers fell to their deaths from the roof of the grandstand, and the falling debris also took the life of the stage manager. When the action got under way, fan-favorite, Don Branson went out and took the pole position and led every lap of the race to collect his second victory on an Illinois dirt track in as many years.

The racers took to the road for the trip to Milwaukee for the 200-mile race scheduled for the very next day, but it was to no avail. The race was canceled due to rain and held the next weekend. Andretti did it again and started from the pole to win the event despite the constant battle put up every foot of the way from Johncock, who backed off towards the end of the race only because he was running dangerously low on fuel.

In Southern Illinois a week later, three familiar faces were missing when qualifications began for the 19th running of the Ted Horn Memorial. The 1957 winner, Jud Larson, and veteran Du Quoin drivers Jimmy Davies and Red Riegel had all perished in racing accidents earlier in the season.

In the Weinberger Homes Special, Bobby Unser laid down a speed of 105.57 mph to secure the pole position followed by Roger McCluskey. Starting third was defending champion, Branson, with A.J. Foyt – who was experiencing one of his worst seasons of championship racing – in fourth. In fifth was Andretti, who needed to finish seventh or better to pass Johncock, who was still the points leader by a slim margin of 50 markers.

Andretti's chances to accomplish this were excellent as Johncock freely admitted that he didn't feel safe on dirt tracks. He did not race at Springfield and he would not start at Du Quoin. With only three of the 15 scheduled events in 1966 being run on dirt, Johncock was confident he could maintain his lead for the crown.

Bobby Unser (5) grabbed his first pole in Southern Illinois in 1966 while Du Quoin rookie, Roger McCluskey (8) started second and led the first lap before dropping out of the race. Unser then led for 23 laps of the event.

Foyt (2), Branson (4), Knepper (81) and Andretti (1) in the early laps. (The Weatherford/Foutch Collection)

That Magic Mile

Arnie Knepper (81) took the lead from Unser (5) on lap 25 and was in command of the race for the next 64 laps. He dropped out on lap 89 with a faulty magneto. (The Weatherford/Foutch Collection)

Starting sixth was Chuck Hulse, who had not driven at Du Quoin since 1963. Seventh on the grid would be hometown boy, Arnie Knepper, followed by McElreath, Du Quoin rookie Dick Atkins and sophomore driver, Gary Congdon, who rounded out the top ten.

Eleventh was Carl Williams, 12th was Bud Tingelstad, Ralph Liguori would take off from 13th followed by Joe Leonard while Du Quoin rookies, Larry Dickson, Billy Foster, Bob Tattersall and Al Miller completed the field of 18-drivers.

At the drop of the green, McCluskey darted past Unser to lead the first lap of the race as over 19,000 fans cheered. Unser regained control on the second lap as McCluskey, his race over, slowed to enter the pits. Unser held firm until lap 24, when Knepper, who had found that his car handled well enough low on the track to slip past the likes of Foyt, Branson and Andretti, caught Unser on the inside of the north turns and took the lead.

Knepper literally blew-off the field. Even as the yellow flag flew on lap 28, when Andretti's exploded engine scattered parts all over the track, it didn't take Knepper long to regain his comfortable lead over second place Unser.

Knepper would lead the race for the next 60 laps before suffering what must have been sheer heartbreak for the Southern Illinois native. As the magneto on his Central Excavating Special cut out, Knepper had to settle for what was eventually an 11th place result.

The luck of racing, along with some fine and steady driving left Bud Tingelstad in command. The Indianapolis resident, who had started 12th in the Federal Engineering Special was no-better than seventh after 40 laps. After 60 miles, he was fourth and found himself in the catbird seat by lap 83.

Tingelstad led the final eleven laps for his first championship victory. Never threatened, his only challenge might have come from Branson, but that challenge never appeared as Branson headed to the pits on the 91st lap with a blown tire.

In six years of championship competition, the 38-year-old Tingelstad's best finish had been runner up in the 1963 Trenton 200. At Du Quoin, his winning speed of 95.10 mph netted the veteran driver over $5,000 of the $20,000 purse.

In second was Dick Atkins with a fine performance in his first start at Du Quoin. Third was Unser, followed by Leonard, Liguori, and Branson, who had rejoined the race. Foyt, Dickson, Foster and McElreath rounded out the Top 10.

Andretti was credited with a 15th-place finish. It marked the third consecutive year that he would finish in the same position at Du Quoin. Andretti would win three of the remaining four races in 1966 to repeat as the national champion. He became only the seventh driver in the history of national championship competition to be awarded back-to-back titles. In winning eight of the 15 races in 1966, Andretti tied the late Tony Bettenhausen who had won eight of 14 in races in 1951. But A.J. Foyt still held the record. He had gone ten out of 13 in 1964.

Bud Tingelstad led the last 11 laps of the 1966 Ted Horn Memorial and notched the only championship victory of his career. (The Weatherford/Foutch Collection)

The Houston Hustler
September 4, 1967

Despite Mario Andretti's fantastic win behind the wheel of the Holman-Moody Ford at the Daytona 500 in February of 1967, the racing season in the United States opened with a void. Don Branson, whom many considered the penultimate dirt track race car driver had been killed during a sprint car race in November of the previous year at Ascot Speedway in Gardena, California. Also killed in the same accident was Dick Atkins, who had finished second at Du Quoin in 1966.

At the time of his death, Branson had been the all-time starter of USAC championship events after having driven in 126 races. Of those he had been victorious in six. Atkins, who had passed his rookie driver's test at the Indianapolis Motor Speedway only six months before to his death had driven in just 11 championship events, but had already won his first major race. The victory had come at the Sacramento race only days before he died.

The USAC planned a banner year for 1967 and scheduled a record 17 races for the championship trail. By the close of the season a total of 20 events were held. Of these, 10 were run on paved ovals, six more were run on paved road courses while the remaining four were one-mile dirt track events. The addition of the road course events were a further testimony to the ever growing popularity given to the rear-engine race cars. This popularity reached north of the border into Canada and for the first time USAC held races on the scenic tracks of Mosport Park, Ontario and at St. Jovite in Quebec.

Texan, Lloyd Ruby won the first race on the USAC's championship calender - and the third of his career - with a wire-to-wire record setting victory in the 150-miler at Phoenix. In the next event at Trenton a few weeks later he finished dead last, when Andretti won the 150-mile contest from the pole.

*Bobby Unser held down the pole in 1967 for the second time in a row at Du Quoin.
(The Jim Pursell Collection)*

Heading to Indianapolis for the big 500-mile show, Roger McCluskey, the 1966 sprint car champion, had control of the points lead after finishing second in the first two events of the season. But Andretti took center stage after breaking both of his own one and four-lap qualifying records with a speed of 168.982 at the Speedway. Added to this illustrious performance was the fact that it was the first time in the history of the 500 that all 33 drivers would qualify for the race at over 160 mph.

But, the biggest story from the Speedway during the month of May was the introduction of a another new form of racing car by Andy Granatelli, a name now recognized by auto racing fans the world over.

*Roger McCluskey (12) is about to put defending Du Quoin champion, Bud Tingelstad (10), a lap down.
(Southern Illinoisan Photo)*

Granatelli, the president of the fuel and oil additive company known as STP, had been entered as either a driver or car owner at Indianapolis since 1946, but victory had always eluded him. His answer to realizing his life-long ambition of winning the world's greatest automobile race was a car that became known as the "Whooshmobile."

Officially entered as the No. 40, STP Oil Treatment Special, the newly designed car was powered by a Pratt and Whitney turbine helicopter engine incorporated into the left side of the vehicle alongside its driver, the 1963 Indianapolis winner, Parnelli Jones.

At the beginning of the race Jones swept from his sixth-place starting position and was past Andretti and the rest of the frontrunners before the end of the first of 200 laps on the 2.5-mile oval. Jones dominated the race until the 196th lap when a six-dollar bearing failed and sidelined the turbine. A.J. Foyt, who had been almost totally ignored by the press during the entire month of May took the lead. But, the race wasn't over yet.

On the very last lap there was a five-car tangle on the front stretch, but Foyt weaved through the smoking melee at over 50 mph to record his third victory in the Indianapolis classic. Not only did Foyt win the race driving a Coyote, a car he had helped to design and build, he also became the first, and last driver to win the 500-miler in both a front and rear-engined race car.

The Indianapolis victory was the first champ car win for Foyt in over a year and a half. With 1,150 points to his credit, Foyt was well on his way to an unprecedented fifth national driving championship.

That Magic Mile

Al Unser's right-rear tire is changed by Indy car racing's all-time winningest mechanic, George Bignotti. (Southern Illinoisan Photo)

A week later Gordon Johncock won the Milwaukee 100 and Ruby returned to the winner's circle at Langhorne. Foyt finished the two races in 21st and fifth respectively before flying to Europe where he teamed with Dan Gurney in an all-American effort to win the 24 Hours of LeMans. The two drivers won the race driving a Ford GT-40 in the fastest ever LeMans race at an average speed of 135.46 mph. No longer was Foyt just a national hero, he now had a world-wide reputation as one of the best racing drivers in the history of the sport. Gurney, of California, was at that time the only American driver competing regularly on the European Grand Prix circuit. Shortly after the LeMans victory he brought an American made Eagle-Westlake formula one car to the checkered flag at the Belgian Grand Prix. It was the first all-American victory in a Grand Prix race in 46 years.

Back in North America, Bobby Unser won the two races held at Mosport Park and claimed his first two championship victories. Meanwhile A.J. still held a comfortable lead in the points chase, but Mario Andretti would have none of it and won the next four races. They were held at Indianapolis Raceway Park, Langhorne and a twin bill at St. Jovite. Switching to a dirt track for the first time in the season at Springfield, A.J. returned to victory lane as Andretti followed him across the finish line. The little Italian was catching up fast and in the next race on pavement again at Milwaukee he gained another 400 markers for the 200-mile victory. Andretti was just a scant 60 points behind as the championship trail wound its way down into Southern Illinois.

As usual at Du Quoin, the Labor Day racing weekend was hot, sunny and humid. Bobby Unser, driving the Rislone Special for owner Robert Wilke repeated his qualifying performance of 1966 and again secured the pole with a speed of 101.64 mph. Down four miles an hour from the previous year and far off the pace of Don Branson's record speed of 106.038 mph set in 1964.

Starting second was McCluskey just a tick off the pace at 101.21. Third was Foyt, the only other driver to better the 100 mph mark. Jim McElreath was fourth, followed by Ralph Liguori, George Snider and Ronnie Duman. Sitting in eighth was the familiar name of Vukovich.

Many of the 20,000 or so fans thought they were experiencing deja vu when they heard the famous name over the loudspeaker. Looking at the car they saw the name "Agajanian" emblazoned on its side. And the number was the same "98" that his father carried. But it was Bill Jr., at the wheel. A rising star in the USAC ranks, he had already won seven midget races and one sprint car event in 1967.

Ninth would start Al Unser, tenth was another sprint car ace, Larry Dickson, who had won the pole in Springfield. The remaining eight positions were occupied by Andretti, followed by rookie Bill Puterbaugh of Roxana, Illinois. Johnny Rutherford who had broken both arms during a sprint car race in 1966 was returning to Du Quoin after missing the previous year's event. Bruce Walkup was 14th, piloting the only Ford powered entry. Carl Williams was 15th while defending champion, Bud Tingelstad and championship rookies, Norm Brown and Mickey Shaw made up the final three positions on the grid.

As the cars were taking their warm-up laps, the younger Unser, Al, collided with McElreath in the north turn and after a brief delay all 18 cars started the race. At the green, Bobby Unser led into the first turn and had a safe lead heading down the backstretch, but he spun out coming out of the fourth turn and second-place McCluskey took control. Ralph Liguori dropped out on the first lap with a disastrous oil leak. Norm Brown spun out on lap seven and did not rejoin the field. Snider fell out on lap 23 and McElreath followed suit on lap 36. Fourteen cars would finish the race.

For a while it was clear sailing for McCluskey. But the fiery Foyt was keeping pace and the fans could see he was getting closer. After 35 laps they could sense a dogfight as Foyt reached the leader's tail. McCluskey stayed in the high groove as Foyt put his Sheraton-Thompson Special well on the inside of each turn to gain ground.

McCluskey withstood the pressure until the 44th lap when Foyt finally got past. Andretti, who had slowly improved on his 11th place start passed McCluskey on the 48th trip around the oval and set his sights on Foyt.

That Magic Mile

But Andretti and his Dean Van Lines Special were no match for Foyt as the latter drew away to a half a lap advantage and cruised to an unprecedented fifth victory on the Magic Mile and the 35th of his career.

The winning speed of 93.58 mph was slowed by the few yellow flags that appeared during the race, but the race record of 97.80 mph set by Foyt in 1964 remained in place.

Behind Andretti finished McCluskey in third with Dickson, Vukovich, Bobby Unser, Tingelstad Carl Williams, Al Unser and Ronnie Duman made up the top ten.

Of the six remaining races of the 1967 season Foyt would win two and finish in the top five on two different occasions to lock up his fifth National Championship in the closest points battle in the USAC's history. Andretti won two more events that year and ended his season just 80 points behind Foyt.

A.J. Foyt became Du Quoin's grand champion with his fifth victory in 1967. (Courtesy of the Indianapolis Motor Speedway)

Mario A Go-Go
September 2, 1968

The 1968 National Championship season opened with a packed schedule of 27 events. New races were added on road courses at Las Vegas and Castle Rock, Colo., and on the recently constructed Michigan International Speedway's two-mile oval. The USAC awarded a third event to Langhorne, but the good news for dirt car fans was the sanctioning of a fifth dirt car race at Nazareth, Penn., the adopted hometown of Mario Andretti.

During the off-season, Andretti had purchased the entire Dean Van Lines racing stable from the estate of its late owner, Al Dean. Andretti retained most of the team's staff including mechanics Clint Brawner and Jim McGee. Like Foyt, Andretti had now become one of the few owner/drivers in USAC Championship competition.

The action started at Hanford, Calif., where Gordon Johncock won the 200-miler for the second year in a row. Bobby Unser took victories in the next four events at Las Vegas, Phoenix and Trenton along with his first Indianapolis 500 crown. He would win the 500 again in 1975 and 1981.

In the 500, Unser, starting third and driving an Eagle chassis powered by a turbo-charged Offenhauser engine defeated the three STP turbines entered by Andy Granatelli. Losing again was the last straw for Granatelli, and while he would again enter cars in the 500, the turbines would never appear at the Speedway again.

As the racers arrived in Milwaukee for the traditional race after the 500, Unser held a healthy 885-point lead over Lloyd Ruby, the eventual winner of the 150-mile Wisconsin State Fair event.

But it seemed that Unser had fallen under the mysterious "Indy jinx" that has plagued the winners of the 500 through history. Few winners of the past had successful seasons after being victorious at the Speedway.

*Al Unser sat on the pole in 1968 with a speed of 98.10 mph.
(Courtesy of the Indianapolis Motor Speedway)*

He finished 18th and out of the points at Milwaukee. Then in Toronto he took a wild off-course ride in the first race of Mosport's twin 100-milers that resulted in minor injuries and a destroyed race car that caused him to miss the second event. Dan Gurney won both Canadien events while Unser again collected no points.

In the next event, the first of the season's three at Langhorne, it was Johncock again in the winner's circle, but Unser did finish second and claimed 240 markers.

At Castle Rock, he could fair no better than 11th place to collect just 30 points while Foyt appeared in victory lane for the first time on the championship trail in 1968.

Lloyd Ruby attempted to qualify the rear-engined Gene White & Company Special on the Du Quoin dirt in 1968, but failed to find enough speed. (Southern Illinoisan Photo)

The next event of the season was the inaugural running of the 100-mile dirt race at Nazareth. It was the first race ever run at night for the USAC champ cars. Billy Vukovich, the Indianapolis 500 Rookie of the Year, sat on the pole for the first time in a big car. Al Unser snagged the lead on the first lap and held off the hard-charging hometown driver, Andretti, every step of the way to score his first ever championship victory. By the time the twin 100-mile races were run at both Indianapolis Raceway Park and at Langhorne, Al had completed an amazing string of five victories in a row. Only Foyt had assembled a better record when he won seven consecutive events in 1964. Al now trailed big brother, Bobby, in the points while Andretti was a very close third.

The next two races in Quebec at St. Jovite went to Andretti. Returning to the dirt at Springfield, Roger McCluskey came out on top as did Ruby on the pavement in the second of the season's two races at Milwaukee. But, the points scenario remained the same with Bobby Unser, Al Unser and Mario Andretti still running one, two and three as the Indy car series headed for Du Quoin.

A total of 29 drivers began their qualifying attempts as the sun rose toward its zenith over Southern Illinois, guaranteeing a long, grueling day for the drivers and team members in the pits.

Al Unser's flying speed of 98.10 mph in the No. 5 Retzloff Chemical Offenhauser insured him of the pole position as Du Quoin sophomore driver, Bill Puterbaugh, turned in a 98.04 for second position on the starting grid.

Puterbaugh, of Roxanna, Illinois had finished 16th in the Sprint Car ranks and 73rd in the Midget Car standings in 1967. Now, he was having a promising, but limited season in the big cars. He had placed in the top 10 in five of the six races he had qualified for in 1968 driving for several different car owners. Today's mount was the No. 77 Dayton Steel Wheel entry. Puterbaugh would become a local favorite at Du Quoin for many years to come.

Nailing down third position was Foyt, looking for his sixth win in Southern Illinois. Despite just one victory in 1968, A.J. was carrying the distinction of being the first millionaire racing driver ever to compete at Du Quoin. In the space of a 12-year driving career, Foyt had finally topped $1,000,000 in racing earnings.

Fourth came the second generation Vukovich. He stood fifth in the championship points and had led several laps this season in the big cars. He had won in the sprints and midgets - with one of the former victories coming at Du Quoin in 1967 - and was hungry for a National Championship first.

Fifth was points leader, Bobby Unser, in the No. 3 Risilone Special with Andretti just a split second behind. Seventh was Bruce Jacobi in his second start at Du Quoin, followed by Carl Williams, who was making his fourth start on the oval. Ninth was Roger McCluskey as Jim Malloy occupied 10th driving the only Ford powered car in his rookie year.

Next came Jerry "Scratch" Daniels, another driver making his first start at Du Quoin. Daniels had failed to qualify for the 1967 Ted Horn Memorial and this year would drive the single Chevrolet powered car. In 12th was another rookie driver named Tom Bigelow, of Whitewater, Wisconsin. Bigelow would compete at Du Quoin for the next 25 years.

George Snider would begin the race in 13th followed by Art Pollard with Ralph Liguori on the inside of the eighth row. Next to Liguori in the 16th spot was the familiar name of Bettenhausen.

When the 18,400 fans heard the name, Gary Bettenhausen, over the public address system they went crazy. Here in person was the second running of the "Tinley Park Express." They had heard of his exploits in the midget, sprint, stock and big car ranks, but many had never seen the oldest son of the three-time Du Quoin champion. Like Bigelow, Gary Bettenhausen would race in Southern Illinois for the next quarter of a century. But today he would leave a lasting impression on the fans

Al Unser leads the field in the No. 5 Retzloff Chemical Special at the wave of the green flag. (The Weatherford/Foutch Collection)

Billy Vukovich shot from fourth place to first just after the start and led the first six laps. (Southern Illinoisan photo.)

Belleville's Arnie Knepper sat on the inside of the last row and rookie George Benson rounded out the field as the list of non-qualifiers grew. These included former winner, Bud Tingelstad, while talented drivers Larry Dickson, Rollie Beale, Wally Dallenbach, Greg Weld, Bobby Grim, and Lloyd Ruby failed to make the cut.

Of note was the failure of Ruby, who stood fourth in the points behind Andretti. Ruby had failed in an attempt to put the rear-engined Mongoose-Drake Turbocharged Gene White Special into the lineup. It was the same car that had brought Ruby victories in both of the season's Milwaukee races, but as proved before, a rear-engined machine was just not competitive on dirt.

Young Vukovich busted loose when he saw the green waving as he exited the fourth turn on the pace lap. Taking the higher groove of the track he shot by Foyt, Puterbaugh and Al Unser and emerged as the leader with one lap into the record book. Remaining on the high cushion of the track, Vukovich built up a sizable lead until his steering wheel went rigid in his hands at the end of six laps. Realizing he had lost the power steering in his Wagner Lockheed Brake Fluid Special, Vukovich fought to regain control as he cut down to the inside. Andretti, who had also battled his way past Foyt, Puterbaugh and the Unser brothers, was on the outside and right behind the surprised Vukovich. Andretti shot into the lead.

That Magic Mile

Andretti piled on the speed and by lap 21 he had lapped every driver except Vukovich, Foyt, the Unsers and Roger McCluskey. As he enjoyed his six-second lead over Vukovich, Andretti may have had time to remember back to 1961, when he competed in his first open cockpit race behind the wheel of a former Ted Horn-driven sprint car that had won five AAA championships. Now, seven years later, Andretti was finally leading the race named after the great champion.

On lap 24 Bobby Unser was hit by the "Indy jinx" again as his car slowed with electrical problems. He would receive no points today, but even more devastating was the fact that if Andretti indeed came out as the winner, he would gain another 200 points toward the title.

Mario maintained a strong lead over the field as Ralph Liguori lost his brakes seven laps later. Knepper's engine blew on the very next lap to slow the field, but at the halfway point Andretti again possessed a comfortable advantage.

Behind him, Foyt had crept up on Vukovich and took second place briefly as the two drivers battled furiously with McCluskey and Al Unser for position. Bruce Jacobi took a wild spin in the third turn to bring out the yellow for four laps that bunched up the 15 remaining cars.

When the "go flag" appeared it was much of the same. Andretti held his lead as Al, A.J., Vukovich and McCluskey dueled. As the four bottled up behind the lapped car of George Snider, Gary Bettenhausen made tracks to stay close to the leaders. He had come from 16th on the grid and was now in sixth.

On lap 62 Foyt took the runner-up spot and set his sights on Andretti. McCluskey settled into third followed by Al Unser and Vukovich while Bettenhausen and Bigelow were a lap down in the sixth and seventh positions.

On the 70th lap Art Pollard smashed into the guardrail of the north turn. Pollard was not hurt seriously, but the accident brought out the yellow flag for the next 14 laps.

At the drop of the green Foyt, charged and lap after lap began to whittle away at Andretti. Thirteen laps later McCluskey blew a tire and coasted to the pits. It was now Al Unser in third with Vukovich on his tail and pushing hard. Bettenhausen stayed a lap down, but had graduated to fifth place.

Foyt and Andretti were neck and neck for the next five laps. Unser's right rear could take no more and started to loose air as Al headed in for a costly tire change. This left the lead lineup of Andretti, Foyt and Vukovich in place for the last few laps. The crowd was on its feet enjoying a thriller of a finish as Andretti barely crossed the finish line ahead of A.J.

Andretti collected $5,696 for the victory. But, more importantly was the fact that he was in striking distance of Bobby Unser's points lead. Mario now stood just 792 points behind with seven races left on the schedule.

The 1968 season ended with the closest points fight ever between two drivers. A.J. Foyt won the following race at the Indiana State Fair as Andretti came in second after flying back from Italy where he had practiced for the Italian Grand Prix less than 24 hours before. Bobby Unser finished out of the points in 16th. In the next race at Trenton, Andretti was victorious and cut Unser's point margin to 283. Foyt won again at Sacramento as Andretti cruised to fourth and another 120 clickers.

A week after his Formula One debut at Watkins Glen, N.Y., in the United States Grand Prix - where he took the pole, but retired early - Andretti finished second in the inaugural race at Michigan International Speedway. Andretti took a 132-point lead over Bobby Unser, who ended in 17th. Neither driver would win again in 1968 as A.J. Foyt, Gary Bettenhausen and Dan Gurney would claim the last three races. But Unser, with the mark of a true champion, battled back with a fierce determination to overcome his bad luck streak. He finished in second in the last race at Riverside, Calif., to best Andretti by a mere six points for the National Championship title.

Mario Andretti (2) took over the lead on lap seven and held it all the way. A.J. Foyt (1) stayed right on his tail during the later stages of the race. (Southern Illinoisan Photo)

That Magic Mile

Mario Andretti talks to the crowd after his victory as Tony Hulman looks on. (Southern Illinoisan Photo)

Big Al
September 1, 1969

The inaugural running of a 500 mile race was now scheduled for the day before Labor Day in 1970 at the Ontario Motor Speedway in Southern California. Not surprisingly, many dirt car fans were concerned that the 1969 running of the Ted Horn Memorial at Du Quoin would be the last. But Merle Jones, the sports editor of The Southern Illinoisan, reported that no plans had been made by Bill Hayes, the president of the Du Quoin State Fair, to cancel the event.

Henry Banks, the USAC's Director of Competition, assured all those concerned that Du Quoin would still have its championship race, but that it may have to be rescheduled. At the same time, Banks also indicated that the USAC was considering starting a special series for the big dirt cars. While he gave no date for the beginning of a new series, it was obvious that it was now just a matter of days before the National Championship would be contested by only rear-engined race cars on paved venues.

As the 1969 season opened in the Arizona desert, Al Unser grabbed the first pole of the season but championship rookie, George Follmer, a successful sports car racer, surprised everybody when he ran away with the Ford dominated Phoenix 150 in a Chevrolet powered machine. Mario Andretti, who finished 16th in the event got on track at the Hanford 200 and gained 400 points with the win to open what would eventually become a dream season for himself and his car owner, Andy Granatelli. Andretti led every lap of the race from the pole and gave Granatelli his first ever championship victory after a quarter of a century in the sport.

At Indianapolis, Andretti came back after a terrifying pre-race practice accident that demolished his four-wheel drive Lotus, and put his Hanford winning Brawner Hawk in the No. 2 starting position next to polesitter, A.J. Foyt, who was gunning for his fourth Indy title. After

Defending Ted Horn Memorial champion, Andretti, consults with car owner, Andy Granatelli.
(Southern Illinoisan Photo)

That Magic Mile

Greg Weld is interviewed after securing the pole at Du Quoin in 1969. It was the second of four straight dirt track pole positions Weld would claim that year in the Plymouth powered No.60 STP Gas Treatment Special. (Southern Illinoisan Photo)

holding off both Foyt's and Lloyd Ruby's challenges during the first half of the race, Andretti cruised to a long overdue victory for himself, Granatelli and chief mechanic, Clint Brawner, who had been trying to wrench a win at the Speedway for more than a decade.

In the following Milwaukee race after a 10-car accident on the first lap, Art Pollard, Andretti's STP teammate won his first championship victory and handed Granatelli his third win in a row. Mario would finish in seventh.

Andretti's dry spell continued through the next two races as Bobby Unser won at Langhorne and Gordon Johncock took top honors at Castle Rock, Colorado after a furious battle with the defending champion, Foyt.

Mario's magic returned in his hometown of Nazareth, Pa., when he won the first dirt track event of the season. It continued on to the peanut shaped Trenton oval where Andretti recovered from a near disastrous flat tire and wrestled a victory from Wally Dallenbach.

In the twin 100-milers at Indianapolis Raceway Park, Andretti posted second and ninth place finishes behind the road racing stars, Dan Gurney and Peter Revson.

At the second Milwaukee race of the season on Indy car racing's "Monster Mile," Al Unser began his dramatic surge from nowhere in the 1969 season after leading almost every lap from start to finish in the 200-mile event that saw Al beat his brother, Bobby, across the finish line.

The youngest of the racing Unser brothers had started the season on a promising note when he signed as the lead driver for the revamped Parnelli Jones/Vel Miletich team. Finishing 22nd and 13th in the first two races of the season, the newly formed team, with famed mechanic George Bignotti on board continued to gel together when practice began for the Indianapolis 500. Al consistently posted fast speeds during practice. But, while celebrating his birthday on the eve of qualifications and performing wheelies on a motorcycle on the Speedway's infield, Unser suffered a broken left leg. The doctor's prediction was that he would be out of competition for at least four months.

Surprisingly, Unser was driving a race car again in just over five weeks. He finished ninth at Castle Rock, sat out the dirt event at Nazareth and was 25th at Trenton. Then, he scored second and 19th place finishes in Indianapolis Raceway Park's double bill before hitting victory lane at Milwaukee.

Al Unser is ready to qualify the No.3 Vel's Parnelli Jones dirt car. (The Jim Pursell Collection)

Johnny Rutherford would start 12th in his fifth appearance in Southern Illinois. (The Fred Huff Collection)

Greg Weld's engine began to overheat even as he led the field to the green flag, but he still managed to stay in the race for 31 laps. (Southern Illinoisan Photo)

That Magic Mile

Mike Mosely, in the Zecol-Lubaid Special hit the guardrail on the eighth lap and rolled his car. He was not injured.
(The Weatherford/Foutch Collection)

The very next day at Springfield, Andy Granatelli unleashed the 1967 USAC Sprint Car Champion, Greg Weld, in the highly anticipated Plymouth powered STP Gasoline Treatment Special. Weld would secure the pole for the race at three mph faster than his teammate, Andretti, the lead STP driver. Mario would start second in a traditional Offenhauser powered car. Weld lasted just 20 laps before frying his motor. Andretti took the victory and immediately flew to Des Moines, Iowa to be with his twin brother, Aldo. He had been seriously injured the day before while competing in a non-USAC sprint car race.

Next on the schedule was the race on the steeply banked and ultra-fast Dover Downs one-mile speedway in Delaware. Art Pollard nailed another victory for Granatelli and moved to seventh in the points standings. Of interest here was the 11th and 12th place finishes of Mario Andretti and Al Unser. A week previously, Unser had not even been included in the points standings of the top 20 drivers of the 1969 season. But, with 690 points largely earned with the 400 clickers he had claimed at Milwaukee, he was now situated in 11th place. Andretti was first with 2,965 followed by Bobby Unser, who possessed 1,545. With about 3,000 points available to the winners of the remaining ten races on the schedule, the mathematical possibility that Al Unser could catch Andretti was there.

At Du Quoin, Weld grabbed his second of four straight dirt track poles after tooling around the oval at better than 105 mph. Again, he would have Andretti to his right in the second starting position in front of 14,077 spectators.

In third was Bobby Unser in the Bardahl Special with Roger McCluskey on the outside in Foyt's old Sheraton Thompson car, now racing as the No. 82 G.C. Murphy entry. Fifth was A.J. in his new Ford powered No. 6 looking for his sixth win in Southern Illinois. To his right was Du Quoin rookie, Mike Mosely, who had advanced from the sprint car division after posting three victories. Mosely's best showing in his two years of competition in the National Championship series was a third-place finish in the 1969 Trenton 200. He had finished eighth in his rookie year in the 1968 Indianapolis 500.

Starting seventh would be Billy Vukovich while Gary Bettenhausen grabbed eighth on the grid. Ninth was Bill Puterbaugh and Larry Dicksen rounded out the top ten.

Filling out the 18-car field was Al Unser - also equipped with Ford power - followed by Johnny Rutherford, George Snider, Jim McElreath Jerry Daniels, Arnie Knepper, Tom Bigelow and Sam Sessions, the second Du Quoin rookie in the field. Sessions' best previous showing in National Championship competition was a ninth place finish in the 1968 Indianapolis 500.

In the closing laps it was an all Al Unser (3), Andretti (2) and Foyt (6) show. (Southern Illinoisan Photo)

Flagman Shim Malone observed a good deal of sprinting as the cars approached the start/finish line, so he delayed waiving the green banner and made the drivers circle the track again in order to line up in proper formation. Weld pulled over to talk to his chief mechanic, Grant King, about what turned out to be too rich of a fuel setting. Malone started the race and the defending national champion, Bobby Unser, was off and running from the second row with Andretti right on his tail. As the cars completed the first lap Foyt was in third followed by Vukovich, Al Unser, Weld, Puterbaugh and McCluskey. Rutherford and Bettenhausen had brushed the guardrail and each driver headed to the pits to check for damage. Both drivers returned to action.

The order remained the same until Mosely experienced the day's only serious accident and rolled his car on the eighth lap. Malone's yellow

That Magic Mile

flag waived for the next 10 laps as Mosely was removed uninjured and his car was towed from the track.

When the green flag flew again the first 10 positions were occupied by Bobby, Mario, A.J., Vukovich, Al, McCluskey, Snider, Dickson, Knepper and Weld, who's car was trailing wisps of smoke and obviously in trouble.

Foyt, looking to notch his 42nd championship victory began to move. Bobby and Mario had not been as quick since the drop of the green and A.J. was making hay now, reeling in both Unser and Andretti lap after lap. Foyt's red leather gloves could be seen furiously sawing at the steering wheel as he kept his car low on the track. Unser and Andretti used the high groove. On the 30th lap the Texan made his move and drove under the two leading cars to take the lead.

Meanwhile, Al Unser had charged from 11th place and was nipping at the heels of the lead pack of cars. After dicing with Vukovich he disposed of his older brother on lap 39. The stage was set for the finish even though there were still 61 miles remaining.

Foyt's lead was getting stronger. He had built an advantage of almost seven seconds over the field. Mario was second hoping for a rare Foyt mistake while Al looked for an opportunity as well. He found it soon and shot past Andretti. The only Ford powered cars in the race now ran one and two.

On lap 31, Weld's STP Plymouth finally succumed to overheating and he retired. Next down was McCluskey on lap 57 when his gear box failed and slowed the race for the next five laps under the caution flag.

When the green flew once more Unser began his dash and started to whittle away at Foyt's lead. But A.J. began to turn the fastest laps of the race before slipping back on lap 79. Unser closed in for the kill.

As the three leaders headed down the back stretch on the 92nd circuit, Jerry "Scratch" Daniels, running a lap down, was out of fuel and about to be passed again. As he exited the fourth turn he held up his hand to warn the other drivers that he was about to drop down and head to the pits for gas. What Daniels didn't know was that he was heading right into the path of Foyt.

Foyt breaked hard and somehow swung around. Al did the same. Mario closed in. As the the 93rd lap began the fans jumped to their feet and watched Foyt, Unser and Andretti - with the nose of his car barely in the lead - dragrace down the front straight. The three drivers fought for position the entire lap thrilling the fans. But it was Unser with the superior Ford power over Andretti's Offy that took the lead. Foyt pushed hard only to lose ground in the corners.

Foyt never recovered and Unser went on to beat Andretti by just one car length for his first victory at Du Quoin. A.J. was third, followed by Vukovich and Bobby Unser.

Al would collect $5,907 of the total purse of almost $25,000 for his thrilling victory and another 200 chips toward the longshot of catching Andretti's title pot. And, with his Ford powered car, Unser would post the first Ted Horn Memorial victory ever with an engine other than an Offenhauser.

With nine races remaining in the season Unser put forth a noble effort in the chase for Andretti. Standing behind Mario in 10th place (3,125-890), Unser would eventually displace his brother Bobby for second place in the points and finish 5,025-2,630 after the season finale in the Riverside 300.

Andretti's memorable season ended in triumph with the victory in California (where Al Unser finished second). The great driver had clinched his third National Championship and had finally arrived in Victory Lane at Indianapolis. He was now at the pinnacle of American open wheel racing, but there was more to come. In less than 10 years he would become only the second driver from the United States to become a World Champion Grand Prix driver. A feat no other American racer has since accomplished.

*Where's Al? The winner is surrounded by fans after a thrilling victory in 1969.
(Southern Illinoisan Photo)*

That Magic Mile

The Marlboro Man
September 7, 1970

Al Unser's 1969 season would act as a catapult for 1970. Winning three of the last nine races in 1969, the Johnny Lightning pilot added a side trip to Indy in late October and turned the fastest unofficial laps ever run at the Speedway. At over 172 mph, Unser used the practice time as a preview of what was to be expected of him and his team the following season. For good measure, car owner Miletich instructed Unser to put his motorcycle into storage for the month of May.

The USAC opened its 15th season of National Championship competition, now known as the Marlboro-USAC Championship Trail at Phoenix on March 3. The first of 22 events that would be contested in 12 different states was struck like a bolt of lightning by Unser and his Topper Toys sponsored team.

With the advice of Parnelli Jones, the preparation of equipment by Bignotti and the driving abilities of Unser, the USAC record books would be rewritten like never before.

Andretti sat on the pole at Phoenix and got off to his usual good start, but Al would take over for good on the 15th lap and eventually defeat his older brother by 28 seconds at the end of the 150-mile event.

A pair of third place finishes at Sears Point, California and Trenton put Al securely in the points lead as the teams headed to the windy and rain-soaked Indianapolis Motor Speedway for the 54th running of the 500.

As expected, the 31-year-old Unser won the pole with a qualifying speed of 170.221 mph, but Johnny Rutherford surprised everyone when he turned in an average speed of 170.213 in his Patrick Petroleum Eagle. Foyt would start on the outside of the front row.

Prior to qualifications in 1970, Andy Granatelli and Dan Gurney discuss engine performance.
(Photo by Don Figler)

The 1970 starting lineup was the fastest in the Speedway's history with an average speed of 167.139. Unser went on to win his first 500 after leading all but 10 laps of the event. He became the first driver since his car owner, Jones, who in 1963 won the race from the pole. Unser also became the first driver ever to take home over a quarter of a million dollars for a 500 victory. On top of that, Al was now sided with the 1968 winner, Bobby Unser, as the only brothers ever to win at the Speedway. As an added bonus, the younger Unser would travel to the next race at Milwaukee with a 790-point margin over second place Dan Gurney in the Marlboro Championship standings.

At the following event, the Rex Mays 150 in Milwaukee, Unser slipped into the inherent "Indy's Winner's Jinx" and finished third. But teammate, Joe Leonard, the fromer three-time National Motorcycle Champion, driving the team's other Johnny Lightning Special won the race after defeating Roger McClusky by 4.5 seconds.

The Langhorne 150 turned into sibbling rivalry all the way to the checkered flag as Bobby Unser took the pole and led early on. Al took the lead late in the event and looked like a sure bet, but Mom Unser's oldest Indy 500 winning son nipped his baby brother by a scant .73 of a second to score his single victory during the 1970 season.

Likewise, Andretti would win his only race of the year at the Castle Rock, Colorado road course despite a record setting pole position start from Al Unser. Andretti would log the 31st victory of his champ car career as Al would come in fifth.

Gary Bettenhausen was the next winner on the Marlboro Trail when he notched his second career victory in the 200-miler on the high banks of Michigan International Speedway. Unser would finish a miserable 18th after a blown right rear Firestone damaged his car so badly that he completed just 28 laps. Al must have thought that he would never shake the Indy jinx despite the 890 point lead he held over his brother. With a second place finish at Michigan, Bobby Unser had relegated Andretti to third in the standings by only 15 points.

Al's bad luck lifted after the rainy 150-miler on the road course at Indianapolis Raceway Park in Clermont, Indiana. After surviving two spin outs and a "splash and dash" pit stop for fuel with just two laps remaining, Unser found himself with a comeback victory that washed away any bad luck he may have had for the rest of the season.

With almost a month off, the drivers were back on the championship trail and met at Springfield for the first of the five dirt track events of the season.

Because of the rains that had drenched the Illinois capital the race day schedule was delayed and qualifications were called off. As a result, 27 drivers - at that time the largest field ever for a championship dirt track event - drew for their starting positions.

The Springfield race of 1970 was a mudbath that saw only seven cars finish the marathon event. Al Unser won after starting sixth. His winning average race speed of just 62.30 mph was the slowest posted for a 100-mile championship dirt race since Eddie O'Donnell was victorious on Southern California's one-mile Ascot Park track in 1915. The winning speed of that race had been 59.10 mph.

The next day at the second Milwaukee race of the year, the scenario changed. Al, the pole sitter, ran a flawless race under green flag conditions and logged a record race speed of just over 114 mph in the 200 lap event. The New Mexican driver scored his 16th career victory since his debut as a championship contender on the very same track in 1964.

Again, his brother and Andretti failed to finish a race. So as the Championship Trail headed west for the second 500-mile race of the season at the "Big O" at Ontario, California, Unser held a comforting 1750 point lead in the Marlboro-USAC standings.

A rare mechanical problem forced Unser out of the race while on the 186th lap as Jim McElreath scored his fifth victory in 117 championship starts piloting a Coyote Ford entered by A.J. Foyt.

The drivers caught their respective flights to St. Louis that evening in order to make it to Du Quoin the next day. Al Unser was virtually assured of winning his first national championship title with a lead of 1,610 points over the now second place McElreath (1,880). Andretti was still in third with 1,635, followed by Bobby Unser (1,540), Mike Mosely (1,210) and Dan Gurney (1,000), who had all but retired from championship competition.

By the close of qualifications for the 23rd running of the Ted Horn Memorial, it was obvious to the more than 14,000 fans on hand that

That Magic Mile

Pole position starter and defending Ted Horn Memorial champion, Al Unser, leads the field to the green flag. (Southern Illinoisan Photo)

they were once again to be treated to another clash of the titans of American open wheel racing. Defending Du Quoin champion, Al Unser, had the pole. In the close to 100 degree heat, Unser laid down the fastest average speed of the day in his electric blue and yellow Ford powered No. 2 Johnny Lightning dirt car. In a chassis constructed by famed dirt car builder, Grant King, and then fine-tuned by Indy car racing's winningest mechanic, Bignotti, Unser clocked a speed of 103.87 mph for the first starting slot. Despite all the talent involved in the qualifying attempt, Unser's speed was far below the standing record run of 106.038 mph posted by Don Branson in 1964.

On the outside of row one was Andretti, also driving a King built chassis, but this year using a Ford powerplant in his red No. 1 STP Special. A.J. Foyt, cruising in his Wally Meskowski built No. 7 Sheraton Thompson and using a Ford engine for the second year in a row, would start third in the lineup.

Oddly enough, the first three starters would begin the race in exactly the same order as they had finished a year ago.

Joining the over 100 mph ranks was Greg Weld with the fastest Chevrolet powered machine. Weld would also pilot a King chassis, but in his case it was the No. 41 car owned by King himself.

Larry Dickson, the soon to be crowned USAC Sprint Car champion rounded out the top five in the second STP car. His qualifying run of 99.69 had been powered by the reliable Offenhauser engine. Dicksen had finished in the top ten in each of his three previous Du Quoin races.

The next driver seeking a share of the record $35,500 purse was Du Quoin rookie, Dick "Toby" Tobias. With a racing career that spannned 20 years, Tobias had just joined the USAC and won his first two sprint car races within the last two months. He had made his championship car debut at Springfield and came in 19th.

Johnny Rutherford had the inside of the fourth row in his No. 18 Patrick Petroleum Kuzma-Offy, while eighth would start another Du Quoin rookie, but one with the very familiar name of Johnny Parsons.

The son of the 1948 Du Quoin winner, 1949 National Champion and 1950 Indianapolis 500 winner, the younger Parsons had decided to follow in his father's tracks and competed in his first USAC event in 1964. After resigning from the Los Angeles police department, he began driving race cars full-time and won his first midget car race in February of 1970. His best championship finish had been a seventh after his first big car race on the Sacramento dirt in 1969.

Ninth came the sprint and midget car regular, Tom Bigelow, making his third start in Southern Illinois. Beside him was Bruce Walkup, also a regular from the sprint and midget ranks. Both of these drivers were considered two of the USAC's brightest young stars. Bigelow had finished in the Top 10 in his two previous Du Quoin races, while Walkup had failed to qualify in 1969 after blowing an engine in practice.

Starting eleventh was George Snider, who had been recognized as an up-and-comer several years earlier by A.J. Foyt. Now a six-time veteran of the Indianapolis 500, Snider had accumulated several Top 10 finishes in USAC championship competition, but to date had not scored a victory in the big cars.

To Snider's right was Mike Mosely, now driving as Bobby Unser's teammate with the Leader Card team. Mosely had recorded two third-place finishes so far in the 1970 season and looked to turn in a better performance at Du Quoin than he had in his first appearance.

In 13th was the part-time Hollywood stuntman, Bob Harkey, who also blew an engine in practice for the 1969 Du Quoin race. Harkey had now qualified for almost 60 championship races since 1963 and had come in eighth in his single appearance in the 1964 Indy 500.

Next was the hard-charging 1969 USAC Sprint Car Champion, Gary Bettenhausen, driving the No. 16 Thermo King Special. Bettenhausen had made his mark in USAC Indy car competition after winning his first race at Phoenix in 1968 and then at Michigan earlier in the 1970 season.

That Magic Mile

On the inside of row eight was Danville's Larry Cannon, a former stock car racer and barber shop owner. Cannon was making his first race at Du Quoin in the big cars after developing a reputation as a winner in the sprint and midget divisions.

To Cannon's right was Bobby Unser, starting from the unlikely position in the second to last row after taking down the pole position in 1966 & 67. No matter, during the course of his sixth race at Du Quoin, the 10 time championship race winner would demonstrate the talents that marked him as one of America's greatest race car drivers.

Seventeenth was Ralph Liguori of Tampa, Florida. Nicknamed "Ralphie the Racer" because of his determined efforts on any race track, Liguori had notched two second-place finishes in the big cars during a 14 year USAC career. In five prior Du Quoin races, his best finish had been fifth in 1966.

Last on the grid was Bud Tinglestad, also a 14-year veteran of USAC racing. During his career Tinglestad had recorded eight top three showings with his single National Championship victory coming on the Magic Mile in 1966.

Failing to qualify was Arnie Knepper for the first time since 1967, when he missed the race while healing from burn injuries. Knepper could not get his Chevy-powered HVK Special up to speed. Nor could the other local talent, Bill Puterbaugh, who struggled with his MVS Ward-Offy. Carl Williams, from Missouri, blew the engine in his Meskowski-Offy during practice and was sidelined for the day.

The Ontario 500 winner, Jim McElreath, had decided to take the day off as did Roger McCluskey. McCluskey was preparing to become the USAC Stock Car Champion in just two more weeks for the second year in a row.

Before the green flag fell Mosely's car was sidelined and out of the race with gearbox failure, and as the race got under way the defending national champion, Andretti, coasted to a halt with a dead engine.

Al Unser was credited with the lead of the race after the first circuit. Foyt was right on his tail with Weld, Dickson and Tobias right behind. Tinglestad, with an overheating engine, was the next driver to fall by the wayside.

The order remained the same for the frontrunners with the exception of Weld, who dropped out of the Southern Illinois classic for the second consecutive year with a fried motor.

Two laps later Walkup called it a day with a broken exhaust system and the next time around Cannon rolled into the pits with faulty ignition wiring. Lap 14 became the last for Parsons. He retired with a severe oil leak and was credited with 10 points for a 12th place showing.

Foyt got the jump on Unser during the next lap and took a commanding lead. For the next 25 miles it would become a cat-and-mouse game between these two great drivers. Again, hard luck struck Johnny Rutherford. He was forced to call it a day on the 42nd lap with magneto failure and finished in 11th place.

It was still Foyt with Unser right behind, while Bobby Unser had suddenly appeared in third after charging from 16th. Fourth was Dickson, who would dice with the elder Unser for the remainder of the race. Bettenhausen and Snider followed in hot pusuit. Liguori was seventh as Harkey, Bigelow and Tobias completed the rest of the ten car field.

When Foyt ran up on lapped traffic, Al zipped past and regained the lead position, but A.J. stuck like glue and continued the duel.

Then on lap 50, the unthinkable happened. Foyt slid high in the third turn after blowing out his right rear Goodyear and flipped his Sheraton Thompson Special. The crowd fell silent as Foyt's car came to rest upside down. It was the first and only time A.J. would find himself in that position during a championship event. As the yellow flag appeared track workers ran out toward Foyt's car which had its front wheel wedged under the guardrail. After a few tense moments, Foyt crawled from the wreck and got slowly to his feet as the crowd gave the grand

Unser led for the first 12 laps before A.J. Foyt (directly behind) took command. (The Fred Huff Collection)

That Magic Mile

With a classic "rim-ride" Unser (2) regained the lead from Foyt (7) on lap 45. (Southern Illiniosan Photo)

*A.J. Foyt found himself in an unlikely position on lap 50.
(Southern Illinoisan Photo)*

champion a five-minute standing ovation. With just minor injuries to his foot, Foyt refused medical care as he was helped from the track.

Meanwhile, Bettenhausen realized he had a broken oil line and his day was done. With the remaining eight car field bunched up after 10 laps of yellow, Al took off and left in a trail of dust. He was never headed again as he fought off the late challenges of his brother and Dickson. Both the older Unser and Dickson were the only drivers to finish on the same lap as Al, who set a new race speed record of 98.155 mph on the way to victory. His race time of 1:01.08 erased the standing mark of 1:01.21 set by Foyt in 1964. The win was worth $8,600 to Unser along with an additional 200 points in his bid as a runaway for the Marlboro-USAC Driving Championship.

Snider was fourth and a lap down in his City of Syracuse Special. Liguori ended his day in fifth, two laps down, and was hospitilized overnight with heat exhaustion. Sixth was Harkey, also two laps off the pace. Bigelow completed 97 circuits for seventh position.

The only other driver left running at the finish was Tobias. He placed eighth and completed 95 laps. But, more important was the fact that Tobias would be the last driver to ever cross the finish line in a race at Du Quoin that would count toward the National Driver's Championship.

In the months following the last championship points paying race on the Du Quoin oval, Unser clobbered all comers and secured the first of the three National Championships he would win in a career that lasted until his retirement in 1994. In the 1970 season, he also won the Hoosier Hundred at the Indiana State Fair and the inaugural race at Sedalia, Missouri, where he clinched the title with ease. But, Unser's season wasn't over yet.

Two weeks later, he tied A.J. Foyt's record of 10 championship victories in a single season with two more wins coming at Trenton and Sacramento on the same weekend. With the final victory in California, Unser also made a sweep of all five championship dirt track races that season.

Al Unser won the last National Championship race at Du Quoin in 1970. (Southern Illinoisan Photo)

Unser would eventually end the season with 5,130 points and bettered the previous single season high points total of 5,025, which was racked up by Andretti in 1969. Scoring points in 17 of 18 races during the 1970 season, Unser also became the all-time single season money earner with a total of more than $500,000. This figure also outdid Andretti, who had banked $363,283 in 1969.

A New Division

Just weeks after the Du Quoin race, the USAC confirmed what had been known by many for some time. In 1971 there would be separate divisions for not just the big front-engined dirt cars, but for road racing cars as well.

As in the past days of the sport, the often large, but many times minute differences between the cars that competed on dirt, paved ovals and road courses had increased to a degree that not even a similar engine could be used for a racing team's three-car program. The expense had become just too much.

The 1971 season saw the USAC run a series of 12 National Championship races on paved oval tracks. Joe Leonard became the first driver to be crowned a USAC National Champion without having to contest a single event on a dirt track. Never mind the fact that the USAC abandoned its earlier plans for a separate road racing series as well.

At Nazareth, Jim McElreath won the first of the four races that constituted the "Championship Dirt Division" as it was called in 1971. He would eventually finish second in the points to George Snider, who would finally win his first big car race at Du Quoin that season. With 22 Indianapolis 500 starts and more than 100 big car races under his seat belt he remains a favorite of the fans at Du Quoin. McElreath, who raced against his son, James, at Du Quoin in 1976 when he finished third, last appeared on the Southern Illinois bullring in 1992.

During the 1970's many of the name drivers of American open wheel racing continued to race on the Du Quoin saucer. Foyt would come back from serious injuries to win again in 1972. Andretti would take the checkered flag in 1973 and again after a furious duel with teammate Al Unser the following year. As time went on the demands of conflicting schedules and as often as not, contract clauses, prevented these drivers from competing in Southern Illinois. They were eventually replaced on the winner's podium by drivers such as Tom Bigelow, who won Du Quoin's first race of the season in 1972 and took victories again in 1975 and 1977. Other winners during that decade included Bubby Jones (1976), Pancho Carter (1978) and Bill Vukovich (1979).

The 1980s became the decade for Gary Bettenhausen at Du Quoin. Winning five of the 11 races (May 1980, September 1980, 82, 83, 88) held on the oval, the 22-time Indianapolis 500 veteran is second only to A.J. Foyt with wins at Du Quoin. Foyt has posted victories six times in Southern Illinois. Bettenhausen, who competed as recently as 1994 at Du Quoin also won what has come to be known as the USAC's Silver Crown Championship in 1980 and 1983.

Rich Vogler won the race in 1981 while Joe Saldana and Rick Hood were victorious in 1984 & 85 respectively.

In 1986 Jack Hewitt won his first of three races in Southern Illinois. The Troy, Ohio native would win again the following year and lock up two consecutive Silver Crown titles at the same time. Still an active participant in many different forms of dirt track racing, Hewitt would win again in 1993 and now approaching his 20th USAC Silver Crown victory, currently holds the record for wins in that division.

Second to Hewitt in Silver Crown victories is Chuck Gurney, of Livermore Calif. A winner at Du Quoin and a Silver Crown Champion in 1989, the highly competitive Gurney won the race again in 1994 and 1996. He continues to be a strong competitor every Labor Day.

In 1990, Jeff Swindell, a World of Outlaws regular, took top honors on the Du Quoin mile. Stevie Reeves won the following year and currently races in NASCAR's Busch Grand National division.

1996 saw the return of Johnny Parsons to the Indianapolis 500 where he finished 28th after a 10 year absence. The long-time USAC veteran won the Du Quoin race in 1992 & 1995 and still holds the current race record on the Magic Mile of 107.047 mph with a time of 56:03.00. Just eight mph faster than the speed of 99.28 mph set by the first Du Quoin winner, Lee Wallard in 1948.

That Magic Mile

And that is just part of the magic of the Du Quoin State Fair's one-mile oval. The fans that continue to pack the grandstand and bleachers year after year every Labor Day know that they will be treated to the same exciting form of racing the fans of years ago experienced. Nothing compares to the noise and color. No one can mistake the excitement of the last day of the fair. Race Day! The fans have seen the best of America's racing drivers travel to Southern Illinois' coal country to compete in the most dangerous of sports.

Between 1948 and 1970, over 400,000 spectators have witnessed 23 National Championship contests in Southern Illinois. Four hundred and fourteen times drivers have qualified for the regions oldest and largest sporting event, which produced 14 different winners. Ten of these drivers earned valuable points on their respective roads to national driving titles. Eight of those winners have combined to win the Indianapolis 500 on 15 separate occasions.

Du Quoin fans have never had to be taught the obvious. They've always known that victory is achieved through a combination of the fastest car, the sharpest mechanic and a talented driver racing on one of the oldest tracks in North America, that Magic Mile.

Acknowlegements

This book would not be complete if the people who offered their valuable assistance were not given credit where credit is due.

First and foremost I would like to thank the late William "Wild Bill" Oldani for planting the seed of this writing in my head on Labor Day of 1991.

Two years later, Southern Illinoisan Newspaper Publisher, Richard Johnston, steered me in the direction of the newspaper's Special Projects Manager, Kevin Bishop, who generously offered not only the use of his office, but also gave me the confidence any writer would need to see his or her work through to completion.

Stacy Faye Bleyer spent much of her valuable time editing this book and has probably re-read it as many times as I have. Hence, she should deservedly be recognized as the Editor in Chief. Also helping out on the editorial side were John Nolan and Larry Davis.

The talented graphic artist, Ian Weidner, was instrumental with regards to the design of this book's cover and undertook the tedious task of the page-by-page layout.

Joe "Bob" Walker, Jay Stemm, Tracey Caraker and J. Scott Hill each contributed equally to solving any technical problems I often encountered while working with unfamiliar computer systems.

When a missing computer file resulted in the loss of every photo caption in this book, Jenny Granados again proved to be a lucky charm and did a first-rate job reconstructing and editing all 98 of them.

Statistically speaking, I owe a great deal to the USAC's Donald Davidson, the Indianapolis Motor Speedway Hall of Fame Museum's Jim Hoggatt and to Carlyn Ewald of the AAA. However, the generous gift by the late Wilson O. Brown of every single USAC Yearbook and newsletter from the years 1956 through 1984 was the icing on the cake.

In the area of photography I am indebted to Phil Harms (who also helped with statistics), Bruce Craig, Terry Weatherford, Keith Foutch, Randall Harbuck C.C.P., Pat Jones of Indy 500 Photos, Dick Carter, Photo Editor of The Southern Illinoisan Newspaper, Don Figler, A.J. Foyt Jr., the late James Scott Pierce, Gene R. Showalter, Jim Pursell, Robert Morefield, Fred Huff and Eugene Gallmeister.

Racing drivers and long time Du Quoin competitors, Randy Bateman and Johnny Parsons contributed driver's insight to this book and I gladly welcomed the views from the cockpits of their racing cars.

Other contributors include: Tom "Gordy" Gorman, Southern Illinoisan Sports Editor – Rick Underwood, Mike Clutts, Dan Dallas, Morris Arnold, Sean Eberly, Steve Fender, Barry Bain, Al Jabr, Dan Pullis, Bob Brown, Anne Fornoro, Bill Hayes, Jane Rader, Roger Karbin, Dave Jacobs, Patty Thompson, Dick Jordan, Chris Duffy and Ron Trentacosti.

Thank you all.

Thomas Nasti